John Greenleaf Whittier's Poetry
An Appraisal and a Selection

John Greenleaf Whittier's Poetry

An Appraisal and a Selection

by Robert Penn Warren

UNIVERSITY OF MINNESOTA PRESS,
Minneapolis

Library of Congress Catalog Card Number: 79-152299
ISBN 0-8166-0605-6

A version of the essay by Robert Penn Warren was first published by The University of the South, Sewanee, Tennessee, in *The Sewanee Review*, LXXIX, 1 (Winter 1971).

To Charles and Doris Foster

Prefatory Note

In printing these selections I have abandoned Whittier's categories and put the poems in chronological order. It seems to me that this arrangement is more likely than his own to indicate something about his development and the relation of the various kinds of poetry to his basic inspiration.

Contents

Biographical Summary

1807 Born December 17, at Haverhill, Massachusetts, second child of John and Abigail Hussey Whittier, the first being Mary, born 1806.

1812 Birth of Matthew.

1815 Birth of Elizabeth.

1826 "The Exile's Departure," Whittier's first poem, sent to the *Newburyport Free Press*, by Mary, and published there by William Lloyd Garrison.

1827 Enrolls at Haverhill Academy.

1828 Becomes editor of the *American Manufacturer*, in Boston, a pro-Clay paper.

1830 Editor of the *Haverhill Gazette*. In June moves to the editorship of the *New England Weekly Review*, at Hartford, Connecticut. Enters literary circles of Hartford; reputation extended. Death of father.

1831 *Legends of New England*, Whittier's first book, published in February.

1832 Return to Haverhill. Ill health and conversion to militant abolitionism by Garrison.

1833 Antislavery pamphlet published, *Justice and Expediency*. Delegate to National Anti-Slavery Convention at Philadelphia; prominent in proceedings as a secretary and member of a committee drafting the Declaration of Sentiments. Beginning of career as agitator and organizer.

1835 Elected to Massachusetts legislature.

1836 Editor of *Haverhill Gazette*; sells family farm and moves to Amesbury.

1837 *Poems Written during the Progress of the Abolition Question in the United States.*

1843 *Lays of My Home and Other Poems.*

1845 Contributing editor to *National Era*, in Washington, where *Margaret Smith's Journal* was to appear.

1846 *Voices of Freedom.*

1849 *Margaret Smith's Journal* and *Poems.*

1850 *Old Portraits and Modern Sketches.*

1853 *The Chapel of the Hermits and Other Poems.*

1857 *Poetical Works.* Death of mother.

1860 *Home Ballads, Poems and Lyrics.* Death of Mary.

1863 *In War Time and Other Poems.*

1864 Elizabeth dies.

1866 *Snow-Bound.*

1867 *The Tent on the Beach and Other Poems.*

1869 *Among the Hills and Other Poems.*

1870 *Ballads of New England.*

1871 *Miriam and Other Poems.*

1872 *The Journal of John Woolman.*

1887 Eightieth birthday a national event.

1888 *Complete Works.*

1890 Death.

John Greenleaf Whittier's Poetry

An Appraisal and a Selection

John Greenleaf Whittier:
Poetry
as Experience

The first Whittier, Thomas, arrived in Massachusetts in
1638. He was a man of moral force, as is attested by
the fact that, a generation before the family had any
connection with Quakers, he took grave risks in protesting
against their persecution.* Despite his espousal of a dangerously unpopular cause, he still had influence in his little world,
and was a holder of office. He was, too, a physical giant and,
at the age of sixty-eight, still vigorous enough to hew the oak
timbers for a new house, the solid two-story structure in
Haverhill where, on December 17, 1807, the poet was to
be born.

At Haverhill John Whittier, the great-grandson of old
Thomas and the father of John Greenleaf, worked a farm of
185 indifferent acres and saw to it that his sons did their
share. John Greenleaf loved the land but loathed the work
on it. For one thing, he was frail and at the age of seventeen
suffered an injury from overexertion; for another thing, he

* The family did not become Quakers until 1694, when Joseph
Whittier, a son of old Thomas, married a granddaughter of one of the
Quakers his father had defended.

3

early had a passion for study. His verses began early, too, and one of them sets forth the intellectual ambition that was to dominate his youth:

> And must I always swing the flail,
> And help to fill the milking pail?
> I wish to go away to school,
> I do not wish to be a fool.

In light of these verses, Whittier's boyhood circumstances, and his admiration for Burns, certain critics have been tempted to think of Whittier, as more than one European critic has thought of Robert Frost, as a "peasant poet." Nothing could be more wide of the mark. The error arises from a confusion to which our contemporary urban, plutocratic society is peculiarly prone: a poor (or even any) farmer is, obviously, a peasant. The Whittiers were farmers, certainly; and if they were not, in relation to time and place, exactly poor, they were not rich. But to think of them as peasants is to fail to realize that what makes a peasant is a psychological rather than an economic fact. The peasant is a member of a fairly rigid and stable subculture that he accepts, fatalistically or pridefully, as the only world in which he can fulfill himself. But when Jefferson thought of his independent farmer, he was not thinking of a peasant; he was thinking of a type central to a whole society. And when the poet Whittier looked backward on the family past he saw the "founding fathers" of a whole new world — a whole society — and if anything characterized his early manhood, it was an almost pathological ambition to take his "rightful" place in that whole society.

The presence, however significant, of folk elements in Whittier's work does not make him a peasant poet any more than the presence of such elements in Faulkner's work makes him a peasant novelist. Indeed, to think of Whittier as a peasant poet is as absurd as to think of Lincoln as a "peasant president." And certainly it is absurd to regard Whittier as a brother to

4

those peasant poets of the eighteenth century in England, such as Mary Collier, the "Poetical Washerwoman," and Stephen Duck, the "Thresher Poet," or John Clare of the nineteenth century, who, when he was patronized in a great house, was set down to his meal with the servants. In one sense, all is a matter of role, and it is hard to imagine Whittier, however full of Quaker meekness, gratefully accepting the role of a guest in the scullery. If he loved Burns, we must remember that when the American quoted "a man's a man for a' that," he held the Declaration of Independence in mind as a gloss.

The house of the Quaker farmer at Haverhill had books, and after absorbing them, the son reached out for others, for Milton, who was to become a personal rather than a poetic model, and such un-Quakerish works as the stage plays of Shakespeare.* Already, by the age of fourteen, Whittier had heard a Scot, "a pawky auld carle," singing songs of Robert Burns at the kitchen hearth of the Whittiers, and in the same year, the schoolmaster, Joshua Coffin, sat in the same spot and read from a volume of Burns, which he then lent to the young listener. "This was about the first poetry I had ever read," Whittier was to say, "with the exception of that of the Bible (of which I had been a close student) and it had a lasting influence upon me. I began to make rhymes myself, and to imagine stories and adventures." It was thus by Burns, and Burns through the voice of the "pawky auld carle," that Whittier's eyes, according to a later account in the poem "Burns," were opened to the land and life around him as the substance of poetry:

* There was no Shakespeare in the little library at the Whittier farmhouse. But even if that library was limited, it was not that of a stupid or illiterate family. Here were, naturally, the Bible, the works of William Penn and other Quakers, and of John Bunyan; various accounts of shipwreck and exotic travel; the multivolume set of Charles Rollin's *The Ancient History of Egyptians, Carthaginians*, etc., translated from the French; Lindley Murray's *English Reader . . . Selected from the Best Writers*; and Sir Walter Scott's *The Pirate*. At an early age Whittier could tell the whole story of the Bible from Genesis to Revelations, and had vast amounts of it by heart. See John A. Pollard, *John Greenleaf Whittier: Friend of Man*, pp. 589–591.

> I matched with Scotland's heathery hills
> The sweetbrier and the clover;
> With Ayr and Doon, my native rills,
> Their wood-hymns chanting over.

But it was not only to nature that Burns opened the boy's eyes. He was already steeped in the legends and folklore of his region, which he had absorbed as naturally as the air he breathed, but Burns interpreted what the boy had naturally absorbed and showed that it was the stuff of poetry. So Whittier, as early as Hawthorne, and earlier than Longfellow, was to turn to the past of New England for subject matter, and by 1831, in a poem called "New England," was expressing his ambition to be the poet of his region. His first volume, a mixture of eleven poems and seven prose pieces, published in 1831 in Hartford, was called *Legends of New England.**

To return to Whittier's literary beginnings, Milton and Burns were not the only models he proposed to himself. There was the flood of contemporary trash, American and English, from writers like Felicia Hemans, Lydia Sigourney, N. P. Willis, the elder Dana, Lydia Maria Child, Bernard Barton, and John Pierpont. The marks of their incorrigible gabble remained on Whittier's sensibility more indelibly than those made by the work of even the idolized Burns; and it is highly probable that Whittier, in spite of the fact that he was to deplore "the imbecility of our poetry," could not nicely distinguish the poetic level of Burns from that of, say, Lydia Sigourney, the "sweet singer of Hartford," who was his friend. He could write, too, of Longfellow's "A Psalm of Life": "These nine simple verses are worth more than all the dreams of Shelley, Keats, and Wordsworth. They are alive and vigor-

---

* Later Whittier was to try to buy up and destroy all copies, but he did reprint an "Extract" in his collected edition. The "Extract" begins: "How has New England's romance fled," and this line tells the whole story of the difference between Whittier's or Longfellow's sense of the past and Hawthorne's. They were drawn merely by the picturesque and anecdotal, Hawthorne by a psychological and moral interest.

ous with the spirit of the day in which we live — the moral steam enginery of an age of action." Whenever "moral steam enginery" came in the door, whatever taste Whittier did happen to have went precipitously out the window. "Strictly speaking," as Hawthorne put it, "Whittier did not care much for literature." * And, if a letter written late in life is to be believed, he cared less for poetry than prose: "I regard good prose writing as really better than rhyme."

But, in addition to all the other poets good and bad that Whittier read, there was, inevitably, Byron. In fact, it was under the aegis of Byron that Whittier, with a poem called "The Exile's Departure," written when he was eighteen, first found his way into print. His elder sister Mary had secretly sent the poem, with only the signature "W," to the *Free Press*, the newspaper at Newburyport. There, on June 8, 1826, it was published — not only published but accompanied by the hope of the editor that "W" would continue to favor him with pieces equally "beautiful."

This editor was William Lloyd Garrison, then only twenty-one, destined to become the most intransigent and famous of the abolitionists. He was also to have a lasting effect on the shape of Whittier's life, but the most immediate effect came when Garrison, having discovered the identity of "W," drove fourteen miles to the Whittier farm, burst in upon the family, and lectured John Whittier on his duty to give the son "every facility for the development of his remarkable genius." To this oratory of a beardless youth, old John Whittier replied: "Sir, poetry will not give him bread."

Nevertheless, the father did allow his son to enroll, one year and some fifty poems later, as a freshman — that is, as a freshman in high school — in the Haverhill Academy, just then established. For two sessions, broken by a stint at school-

---

* As good a proof of this as any is the fact that Whittier found Hawthorne merely a pleasant teller of tales. It is not too hard to believe that Whittier would have instinctively flinched from the inwardness and shadows of Hawthorne's work. In fact, he may have lived only by such a refusal to regard inwardness and shadows.

mastering, Whittier managed to support himself at the Academy, and this was the end of his formal education. By this time his poetry, which issued in a swelling stream, had appeared in distant places like Boston, Hartford, and Philadelphia, and was being widely reprinted by newspaper editors. Whittier was something of a local celebrity, had friends and admirers (whose efforts to raise money for continuing his education at college came to nothing), and was inflamed with ambition and the ignorant confidence that the world was his for the reaching out. He could write that he felt "a consciousness of slumbering powers."

Whittier had already had some experience in the office of the local newspaper, and it was to be through journalism that he entered the great world and became a writer — a pattern very common in America in the nineteenth century but, for various reasons, now rare. Whittier, anxious to take a hand in the "moral steam enginery" of the age, aspired to the editorship of the *National Philanthropist* of Boston, the first prohibition paper in the country, which Garrison had been editing. Alcohol had not proved a worthy challenge to Garrison's mettle, and now he was resigning from the *Philanthropist* to establish, in Bennington, Vermont, the *Journal of the Times*, which was to take as its twin targets slavery and war. Though Garrison sponsored Whittier as his successor in the crusade for prohibition, this did not work out; but the Collier family, owners of the *Philanthropist*, published two other papers, the *American Manufacturer* and the *Baptist Minister*, and did, in 1828, make Whittier the editor of the first.

The *Manufacturer* was a weekly dedicated to the support of Henry Clay and the Whig party, especially to the policy of a high protective tariff. But Whittier, who, while still hoping for the editorship of the *Philanthropist*, had written to a friend that he would "rather have the memory" of a reformer "than the undying fame of Byron," promptly grafted the cause of prohibition onto that of a high tariff, and the

8

first poem he wrote for his editorial column was an un-Byronic ditty entitled "Take Back the Bowl!"

In spite of this and other reformist excursions in the *Manufacturer*, Whittier knew his duty to the Tariff of Abominations enacted in 1828 and the "American System" of the Whigs. As one of Whittier's biographers, John A. Pollard, has pointed out, Whittier, in spite of the fact that he had been raised in the tradition of Jeffersonian democracy, failed to grasp the contradiction between Whig capitalism and his own inherited principles and assumed that what was good for New England loom-masters was good for New England in general and, in fact, for the human race at large. Whittier's Quaker pacifism made him regard Jackson, a soldier and duelist, as the "bloodthirsty old man at the head of our government," and blinded him to some of the economic and social implications of Jacksonian democracy; and so, for some years to come, Whittier continued to believe that Clay, as Pollard puts it, "really was a friend of the common man."

Meanwhile, Whittier helped in preparing a campaign biography of Clay, and came to edit two other pro-Clay papers, the *Gazette* of Haverhill and the *New England Weekly Review* of Hartford. He had made something of a reputation as a partisan editor, with a prose of biting sarcasm and a sense of political strategy. Though the poems poured out in unabated flow, his personal ambitions were more and more political. In fact, it is hard to believe that Whittier was really committed to poetry. The conclusion is not far short of inevitable that he was using his facility in verse as a device for success rather than using poetry as a way of coming to grips with experience. He wrote poems by the bushel and got himself extravagantly praised for them — and why not? He had become a master of the garrulous vapidity which was in general fashion.

But poetry was not enough. The joy of discovery and composition was not enough, nor even the recognition he was receiving. Whittier wanted more than recognition; he wanted some great, overwhelming, apocalyptic success, a success that he probably could not, or dared not, define for himself, a success that would be the very justification for life. "I would have fame visit me *now*, or not at all," he wrote Lydia Sigourney. Again, in a most extraordinary essay, "The Nervous Man," in 1833, he speaks through his character: "Time has dealt hardly with my boyhood's muse. Poetry has been to me a beautiful delusion. It was something woven of my young fancies, and reality has destroyed it. I can, indeed, make rhymes now, as mechanically as a mason piles one brick above another; but the glow of feeling, the hope, the ardor, the excitement have passed away forever. I have long thought, or rather the world hath *made* me think, that poetry is too trifling, too insignificant a pursuit for the matured intellect of sober manhood."

With some rational sense of his own limitations (he knew that what he knew was how to pile the bricks) was paradoxically coupled a self-pity and an air of grievance against the world that had not adequately rewarded the poet, by the age of twenty-five, with that overwhelming, life-justifying, undefinable, and apocalyptic success. So he wrote Lydia Sigourney that politics was "the only field now open." He turned to politics for the prize, not merely by clinging to Clay's coattails, to which he pinned wildly adulatory effusions such as "Star of the West," which became an effective campaign item, but by trying to run for office himself. In this period he made at least two unsuccessful attempts, and a letter soliciting support is significant.

Again, this letter emphasizes the *now*: "It [the election to Congress] would be worth more to me *now*, young as I am, than almost any office after I had reached the meridian of life." And the letter, which in fact was related to some rather dubious maneuvering, shows that Whittier, who had been outraged at Jackson and the spoils system, had secretly learned something — a "something" to which he must now give the moral disguise of unselfishness and loyalty: ". . . if

I know my own heart, I am not entirely selfish. I have never yet *deserted a friend*, and I never will. If my friends enable me to acquire influence, it shall be exerted for *their benefit*. And give me once an opportunity of exercising it, my first object shall be to evince my gratitude by exertions in behalf of those who had conferred such favor upon me. . . ." Which, translated, means: you scratch my back, and I'll scratch yours.

For the moment, nothing came of Whittier's political projects, and nothing came of the love affairs that belong to the same period of his attempt to enter the great world. Whittier, in spite of a certain frailty, was tall, handsome, and attractive to women; and he himself was greatly attracted to women and was rather inclined to insist on the fact. But he remained a bachelor. In the series of love affairs, in the period before 1833, a pattern seems to emerge. The girls were non-Quaker, good-looking, popular, and above Whittier's station, both financially and socially; that is, the choice of sweethearts seems to have been consistent with his worldly and un-Quakerish ambitions. Some biographers take at face value Whittier's statement, made late in life, that he refused matrimony because of "the care of an aged mother, and the duty owed to a sister [Elizabeth] in delicate health." It is true that Whittier's father died in 1830, when the poet was only twenty-three, but his explanation of his bachelorhood does not quite square with the facts; he did not reject matrimony — the girls, with one possible exception, seem to have rejected him.* As an index to wounded self-esteem, frustrated ambition, and a considerable talent for boyish self-dramatization, we have this passage, which, though it dates back to 1828, cannot be without significance in relation to more than poetry: ". . . *I will quit poetry and everything else of a literary nature*, for I am sick at heart of the business. . . . Insult has maddened me. The friendless boy has been mocked

* One girl, Eveline Bray, may not have turned him down, but have been turned down; but if Whittier did turn her down, he apparently did so not for aging mother and ailing sister, but for another girl whom he liked better. See Albert Nordell, *Quaker Militant*.

at; and, years ago, he vowed to triumph over the scorners of his boyish endeavors. With the unescapable sense of wrong burning like a volcano in the recesses of his spirit, he has striven to accomplish this vow, until his heart has grown weary of the struggle. . . ."

There is no way to be sure what went on in Whittier's heart, or in his romances. In 1857, in a poem called "My Namesake," looking back on his youth, he said of himself:

> His eye was beauty's powerless slave,
>   And his the ear which discord pains;
> Few guessed beneath his aspect grave
>   What passions strove in chains.

Though Whittier was aware of the existence of the "chains," we cannot know exactly what they were. It may even be that Whittier, consciously choosing girls that fitted his "passions" and his vaulting ambition, was unconsciously choosing girls who would be certain to turn him, and his Quakerism, down. The whole thing is very tangled, and not less tangled for the fact that, in spite of the courting of non-Quaker girls, he seems to have felt compelled to marry, if at all, within the sect. In 1829, writing about the pretty non-Quaker girls in Boston, he says: "The worst of it is if I ever get married I must marry a Quakeress with her bonnet like a flour dipper and a face as long as a tobacco yawl."

But what was to prevent him from seeking some pretty Quaker girl — or even a pretty Quaker girl who happened to be rich? Such creatures did exist, and the thought of a Quaker sweetheart did cross his mind, for in 1830, in the middle of his love affairs, he wrote a poem to a "Fair Quakeress," and praised her, whether she was real or imagined, for being "unadorned save for her youthful charms," and stated his conviction that beneath the "calm temper and a chastened mind" a "warmth of passion" was awaiting the "thrilling of some kindly touch." But that was as far as he got along this particular line of thought. Whittier did, it is true, have a protracted, complex relationship with one Quaker lady, Elizabeth Lloyd, to whom we shall recur. But this was after he had given up his worldly ambitions and had made, as we shall see, his commitment to abolitionism as a way of life.

The change in the way of life may have made some difference in the kind of girl Whittier, in this second phase, found congenial: poetesses, dabblers in art, abolitionists, hero-worshipers, and protégés. But the old pattern of behavior did not change. In the same period when Whittier had written "The Nervous Man," to which I have already alluded, he composed another remarkable piece of what seems to be undeclared self-analysis; it is called "The Male Coquette," and it is hard not to believe that it predicted the role he was doomed to play until the end.

In any case, there was some deep inner conflict in Whittier, with fits of self-pity and depression, breakdowns and withdrawals from the world, violent chronic headaches and insomnia. A breakdown in 1831 sent Whittier from Hartford and his editorship back to Haverhill, and to such farming as his health permitted. In that period he set about reordering his life, trying to work out a life attitude and a purpose. Here, again, Garrison appeared. Already he had done a hitch in a Baltimore jail (unable to pay a judgment for libelously accusing a shipmaster of carrying a cargo of slaves), had founded, in January 1831, the *Liberator*, the most famous of abolitionist papers, and had written the pamphlet *Thoughts on African Colonization*; and these things had already had an effect on Whittier. Now, in the spring of 1833, Garrison wrote Whittier a direct appeal: "The cause is worthy of Gabriel yea, the God of hosts places himself at its head. Whittier, enlist! — Your talents, zeal, influence — all are needed."

When, a few weeks later, Garrison came to Haverhill and spoke at the Quaker meetinghouse, Whittier was ready now, as he put it, to knock "Pegasus on the head, as a tanner does

13

his bark-mill donkey, when he is past service." Years later, after the Civil War, in the poem "The Tent on the Beach," Whittier wrote, with something less than full historical accuracy, of his shift in direction:

> And one there was, a dreamer born,
>   Who, with a mission to fulfil,
> Had left the Muses' haunts to turn
>   The crank of an opinion-mill,
> Making his rustic reed of song
> A weapon in the war with wrong.

A more candid account appears in a letter to E. L. Godkin, the editor of the *Nation*: "I cannot be sufficiently grateful to the Divine Providence that so early called my attention to the great interests of humanity, saving me from the poor ambitions and miserable jealousies of a selfish pursuit of literary reputation." And from, he added, "the pain of disappointment and the temptation to envy."

Whittier had, apparently, already suffered enough from those things, as well as from other wounds to ego and ambition, and the relief from suffering was what he must have been referring to when, late in life, he said that the question was not what he had done for abolitionism but what abolitionism had done for him.

❧ ❧

Since for more than thirty years abolitionism was the central fact of Whittier's life, it is worth trying to say what it was, and what some of the assumptions behind it were. The difficulty here is, however, that abolitionism had many variants; and to make matters worse, abolitionism, like any vital force, was constantly changing its forms, with bitter factional struggles for power, prestige, and control of policy. But we may best try to understand its essential nature by focusing on the radical variety that is associated with the name of Garrison, remembering that Garrison's own views

14

were not the same from beginning to end. And to understand Garrison's form of abolitionism, or even abolitionism in general, the simplest way to start is to say what it was not.

First, abolitionism was not a general northern doctrine. The abolitionists were always, even during the Civil War, when the emancipation of slaves became a matter of public policy, a minority. In the earlier days, in fact, the mobbing of abolitionists was not uncommon in the North. Garrison himself was manhandled by the "broadcloth mob" of Boston — i.e., well-dressed businessmen — and Elijah Lovejoy was murdered, in 1837, in Illinois. Charles Follen, professor of German at Harvard, lost his post for being an abolitionist, and Governor Edward Everett of Massachusetts, who later was to make the two-hour oration at Gettysburg that preceded Lincoln's two-minute address, asked the legislature for laws to stamp out abolitionism. When, as late as 1862, the Hutchinson Singers entertained the troops of the Army of the Potomac by singing the words Whittier had written to the tune of Luther's "Ein Feste Burg Ist unser Gott," a hymn demanding the end of slavery, the performers were driven out of camp, and one of the Federal officers who helped them on their way was, in fact, reported to have said that he didn't like abolitionists any better than he liked Rebels — a perfectly logical position for a good Unionist.

Second, abolitionism was not anti-racism. If by racism we understand the idea that the Negro (or any nonwhite race) is inherently inferior, then racism was as prevalent in the North as in the South, and the opposition to slavery, whether as emancipationism or abolitionism, had no *necessary* connection with respect for, or acceptance of, the Negro. To dramatize this fact, we may point out that Lincoln, though an emancipationist, did not accept the idea of racial equality. In the light of the general historical and social background, it is not surprising that even an abolitionist *might* be, in one way or another, a racist; but it is true that there was less of

15

this attitude among abolitionists than among the population at large, certainly of the more obvious kind.*

Third, abolitionism was not the same thing as emancipationism. It was a special form of emancipationism. For instance, Emerson, Melville, Lincoln, and Robert E. Lee were emancipationists, but they were not abolitionists. The most obvious difference between emancipationism and abolitionism lay in the intensity of feeling involved, and this difference was associated with the question of contexts in which the problem of slavery might be regarded. For an emancipationist, the problem of slavery, no matter how important it was conceived to be, was to be treated in a general context, social, political, moral, or theological. For instance, Jefferson, in looking to the gradual emancipation of the slaves, placed the problem in a context of social continuity and political stability. And Lincoln, in taking the defense of the Union, not the freeing of the slaves, as the key issue in the Civil War, again considered the social and political contexts. But for an abolitionist the problem of slavery was paramount, central, burning, and immediate. The context did not matter.

Let us glance at this distinction in relation to theology. Behind both abolitionism and the antislavery impulse in general often lay Christian theology. Both the emancipationist and the abolitionist might well regard slaveholding as a sin, but for the latter insofar as he thought theologically, it was the prime and unforgivable sin. Benjamin Lay, a Quaker of the eighteenth century whom Whittier called the "irrepressible prophet," put it this way: "*As God gave His only begotten Son, that whosoever believed in Him might have everlasting life*; so the Devil gives his only begotten child, the *Merchandize of Slaves and Souls of Men*, that whosoever

* Ironically enough, at the fundamental level of mere physical acceptance, there was a great deal less racism in the South than in the North, as the mixture of blood will amply demonstrate, and as many works of southern literature, for instance the novels of William Faulkner, will document. Whittier, like most abolitionists, was opposed to miscegenation.

16

believes and trades in it might have everlasting Damnation." Slavery, according to Lay, was the "greatest sin in the world" — the "very worst part of the old Whores Merchandize, *most filthy Whore of Whores, Babilon's Bastards.*" This particular theological interpretation, by making slavery the "greatest sin," * implied that all other issues had to be strictly subordinated, not only for the benefit of the slave but to save the soul of the abolitionist: if he connives with sin he will be damned. The fear of connivance, furthermore, would rule out any attempt to work at practical solutions such as gradual emancipation or emancipation with compensation (none were, in fact, ever really tried and the elaboration and complication of debate about various schemes may have driven some antislavery people toward the basic simplicity of the abolitionist solution). In other words, a practical solution might be rejected because inconsistent with an abstract point, and this could lead to the rejection of all political action.

Associated with this in the rejection of political action was the notion that slavery was a violation of a "higher law," † of which government and other institutions, insofar as they in any way compromised with slavery, were in contravention. Such a "higher law" cannot, of course, be demonstrated; it can be known only by direct revelation to the individual. So, in a new form, appeared antinomianism, an issue that had plagued Christianity from earliest times and had continued significantly into colonial New England. The antinomian, in the early days of the church, might assume that, because he had received the Christian revelation — "grace" — he could guiltlessly get drunk or commit fornication, and in

* See, for instance, Hawthorne's "Ethan Brand" for a different primary sin.

† This is to be distinguished from the notion that slavery is a violation of "natural rights," though in practice the two notions might lead to the same line of action in defying the state. Here, the proponent of natural law would hold that the state cannot act to abridge natural rights. But the theological notion, with the conviction of personal revelation, gave the cutting edge and the intensity beyond the mere theory of natural rights.

the Massachusetts Bay Colony, Roger Williams and Anne Hutchinson, because of the "Inner Light" and the idea of the inwardness of regeneration, might claim wisdom perhaps superior to that of the Bible, and certainly to that of the synod of churches and the General Court. In any such case, the individual would set his revelation, his conscience, up against the community. This attitude would naturally lead to Garrison's gesture of publicly burning the Constitution as a "league with death and a covenant with hell," and, along with the notion of connivance with evil, to the notion that it was morally wrong even to try to work through institutions. But it must be observed that this is very different from maintaining that it is impractical or impossible to work through institutions. The "pure" Garrisonian might refuse to do so on grounds of principle, but even so, it must be recognized that the attitude toward political involvement was often fluctuating, and at different times, according to circumstances, the same individual might hold different attitudes. For instance, with the rise of the Republican party, a certain number of antislavery people who had previously abjured or despised political action began to accept it.

The notion of "higher law" and antinomianism had another corollary. Since slavery was a sin and a crime, the slaveholder, as a sinner, was denied, and as a criminal was outside of, the protection of law. This line of reasoning might lead to the fomenting of insurrection and the approval of massacre; and did lead to such legends as that southerners liked to use skulls for drinking bowls, a legend in which Harriet Beecher Stowe and even Whittier believed, and which the poet refers to in "Amy Wentworth." More generally the line of reasoning led to the vilification, not only of all southerners, but also of anybody else who failed to accept the abolitionist position, as murderers, thieves, adulterers, and whore-masters, to refer to some of the more amiable charges in vogue. An emancipationist like Lincoln was, to

18

Wendell Phillips, the "slave-hound of Illinois," and even fellow abolitionists might come in for rough handling from those who had nearer relation with the Divine Will: "Among the true, inner-seal Garrisonians," as John Jay Chapman puts it in his sympathetic book on Garrison, "the *wrong* kind of anti-slavery was always considered as anti-Christ." Garrison, that master of vilification, visited as much of his spleen on Frederick Douglass, the ex-slave and fellow abolitionist, as he ever visited on a slave-master.

Abolitionism — at least one brand of it — thus set up against society, squarely and by principle, a naked and absolute individualism. This attitude struck not only at an evil in society, but at the roots of the democratic process, which is based on discussion, the recognition of the contexts of issues, and the assumption that the opponent on any issue is also a member in more or less good standing of society and of the human race; and it was this stripe of dogmatic individualism that Justice Oliver Wendell Holmes, who in 1861 had shared the views of the abolitionists, was to say he "came to loathe" — "the conviction that anyone who did not agree with them was a knave or a fool."

But this very attitude that seems to strike at the root of the democratic process must be recognized as one pole of the democratic process: the claim of the individual intuition to be heard in protest against an order established by a majority, or by vested interests with the toleration of the majority. Clearly, without respect for the criticism arising from the individual intuition there can be no regeneration of institutions. And it is a sadly chastening experience to recognize that rational consensus eventuating in reform is rare, and that the historical process most often involves — and may *necessarily* involve — tragic collisions in which the individual intuition, dogmatically asserted, dynamically dramatizes certain essential values. The whole matter revolves around the question: Is the conscience at any given moment

19

absolute, or is it conceived as less than absolute and, therefore, educable? *

❦

In spite of the fact that many Quakers had been slave-
holders and some, especially the seagoing Quakers of the
southwest of England, had been in the slave trade (there was
an English slave ship of the eighteenth century called *The
Willing Quaker*), the tradition that Whittier directly inherited was that of Benjamin Lay and John Woolman, whose
antislavery writings were fundamental documents in the history of abolitionism.† It was a tradition of brotherhood understood in quite simple and literal terms, and so his entrance into
the abolition movement was a natural act, as was his repudiation of ambition and the reduction of poetry, so dangerously
tied to the physical world and human passions, to the safe
role of a mere "weapon in the war with wrong." But if abolitionism was for Whittier both a catharsis of, and a refuge
from, his ambitions and his passions, the internal tensions in
the movement, both philosophical and practical, set up a
new problem. Whittier spent a large part of his active life
trying to master, resolve, or mediate these tensions. He was
a man of peace and a man of reason, and this world of abo-

* This whole question is a tangled one. The dictates of conscience are, in fact, likely to change from time to time (even Garrison
changed his mind — i.e. his "conscience" — now and then), and in the
face of such a fact how does one pick the moment when he can be
absolutely certain that he is privy to God's will? And if two men of
good conscience disagree, then what? In the ultimate sense, we can
regard the dictates of a man's conscience — even if he himself regards
it as a form of revelation and therefore absolute — as nothing more
than the particular gamble he feels *obliged* to take with circumstances
and history. History (at a certain moment — for history has a way of
changing its mind) may say that the man's gamble was "right"; then
the man gets a statue to his memory. But if history says that the gamble
was "wrong," then the best the man can expect, in lieu of the statue,
is a grudging recognition of his "courage" or "sincerity."
      † Whittier celebrated the "meek-hearted Woolman" in a poem
published in the *Thirty-Sixth and Final Annual Report* of the Philadelphia Female Anti-Slavery Society, 1870, and edited his *Journal*
in 1871.

litionism was no more cut to his measure than the old world he had repudiated. But he survived, and out of the struggle seemed to gain sweetness of spirit. Or did this struggle, by the fact that it absorbed the old struggles of ambition and passion, make possible the sweetness?

و§ §ن

Whittier began his career as an abolitionist in 1833, by writing, and publishing out of his own thinly furnished pocket, a carefully studied and well-argued pamphlet, *Justice and Expediency*, in which he expressed the conviction that the "withering concentration of public opinion upon the slave system is alone needed for its total annihilation." At the end of that year, he attended the convention in Philadelphia that founded the American Anti-Slavery Society, and had an important hand in drawing up the platform, which disavowed all violence and any attempt to foment servile insurrection. All his life it was a point of pride for him that he had been one of the original signers of this "Declaration."

From this time on, Whittier was constantly engaged in the cause of abolitionism, as a writer of both prose and verse, as a member, briefly, of the lower house of the Massachusetts legislature, as an editor of a series of antislavery papers, and as an organizer and speaker. He came to know contumely, the odor of rotten eggs, mob violence, and the struggle against physical fear. He also came to know the formidable wrath and contempt of Garrison.

Whittier had become more and more firm in his belief in political action, that is, in his belief that man is, among other things, a member of society. For instance, in a letter to his publisher, J. T. Fields, he rejected the radical individualism of Thoreau's *Walden*, which he called "capital reading, but very wicked and heathenish," and added that the "moral of it seems to be that if a man is willing to sink himself into a woodchuck he can live as cheaply as that quadruped; but

21

after all, for me, I prefer walking on two legs." * Whittier saw man among men, in his social as well as in other dimensions, and as the proper object of appeal to reason rather than the target for contumely; and nothing could more infuriate the radical Garrison, who was publicly to accuse Whittier of being a traitor to principle. In fact, Whittier, a good Quaker, spent much of his energy, as I have said, in trying to mediate among factions of the movement, an effort that, in the end, came to nothing. The "political" wing of the original American Anti-Slavery Society split off to form the American and Foreign Anti-Slavery Society, and to this Whittier, in spite of his depression over the schism and estrangement from his old friend and benefactor, devoted his energies for some years as an editor, propagandist, and political manipulator. In the last role, his great triumph was to get Charles Sumner to Washington, as a senator from Massachusetts.

As the tensions mounted during the 1850's, Whittier held as best he could to his principles of institutional reform and political action — and to his Quaker pacifism. He never compromised on the question of slavery, but he steadily insisted on viewing the question in human and institutional contexts, as for instance in the poem "Randolph of Roanoke," where he even speaks well of a slaveholder:

> He held his slaves; yet kept the while
>   His reverence for the Human;
> In the dark vassals of his will
>   He saw but Man and Woman!
> No hunter of God's outraged poor
>   His Roanoke valley entered;
> No trader in the souls of men
>   Across his threshold ventured.

When news of John Brown's raid on Harper's Ferry broke, Whittier wrote an article in which he expressed his "em-

*Something of the root impulse that made Whittier reject Thoreau may have led to a revulsion from Whitman so intense that he flung *Leaves of Grass* into the fire.

phatic condemnation" of "this and all similar attempts to pro-
mote the goal of freedom by the evil of servile strife and
civil war" — at the same time, however, he analyzed the
danger which the South created for itself by trying to justify the internal contradiction between freedom and slavery in
his system, and the tension in his feelings is indicated when
he declared, at a meeting called at the time of John Brown's
hanging, that he could not help but "wish success to all slave
insurrections," for an insurrection was — and here he took
a wild leap into a realm of transcendental logic — "one way
to get up to the sublime principle of non-resistance." In other
words, on this test matter of the raid on Harper's Ferry,
Whittier — in his original editorial, at least — agreed with
Lincoln and not with Emerson, Thoreau, Garrison, or the
"Secret Six," the gentlemen who had provided John Brown
with money and encouragement for his project.

There is, in fact, a general similarity between Whittier's
views and those of Lincoln. As early as 1833, in his *Justice
and Expediency*, Whittier pointed out the internal contradiction created by the presence of slavery in the United States,
and declared that "Liberty and slavery cannot dwell in harmony together." He saw the psychological and economic issues raised by this coexistence of free and slave labor. He
held the view that Christianity and civilization had placed
slavery "on a moral quarantine" — in other words, he agreed
with Lincoln that if the extension of slavery was stopped, it
would die out in the slave states without forceful intermed-
dling. Though Whittier had some sympathy with those anti-
slavery people who would resort to a northern secession from
the Union rather than connive in the annexation of Texas,
he fundamentally saw the Union as necessary to the termina-
tion of slavery. As a basic assumption he held the view that
the national problem was to "give effect to the spirit of the
Constitution" — a notion which may be taken to describe
the social history of the United States to the present time.

When the Civil War was over, Whittier saw, as many could

not, that the war had not automatically solved the problem of freedom. Though rejoicing in the fact of emancipation, he could write, in a letter to Lydia Maria Child, that the "emancipation that came by military necessity and enforced by bayonets, was not the emancipation for which we worked and prayed."

❧ ☙

When Whittier, at the age of twenty-six, came to knock "Pegasus on the head," the creature he laid low was, indeed, not much better than the tanner's superannuated donkey. In giving up his poetry he gave up very little. Looking back on the work he had done up to that time, we can see little achievement and less promise of growth. He had the knack, as he put it in "The Nervous Man," for making rhymes "as mechanically as a mason piles one brick above another," but nothing that he wrote had the inwardness, the organic quality of poetry. The stuff, in brief, lacked content, and it lacked style. Even when he was able to strike out poetic phrases, images, or effects, he was not able to organize a poem; his poems usually began anywhere and ended when the author got tired. If occasionally we see a poem begin with a real sense of poetry, the poetry gets quickly lost in some abstract idea. Even a poem as late as "The Last Walk in Autumn" (1857) suffers in this way. It opens with a stanza like this:

> O'er the bare woods, whose outstretched hands
>   Plead with the leaden heavens in vain,
> I see, beyond the valley lands,
>   The sea's long level dim with rain.
> Around me all things, stark and dumb,
>   Seem praying for the snows to come,
> And, for the summer bloom and greenness gone,
> With winter's sunset lights and dazzling morn atone.

But the poetry soon dies, and the abstractions take over and continue relentlessly, stanza after stanza, to the end. Or we see how "Abram Morrison," a shrewd and well-felt character piece, comes to grief through diffuseness and blurred organization.

For a poet of natural sensibility, subtlety, and depth to dedicate his work to propaganda would probably result in a coarsening of style and a blunting of effects, for the essence of propaganda is to refuse qualifications and complexity. But Whittier had, by 1833, shown little sensibility, subtlety, or depth, and his style was coarse to a degree. He had nothing to lose, and stood to gain certain things. To be effective, propaganda, if it is to be more than random vituperation, has to make a point, and the point has to be held in view from the start; the piece has to show some sense of organization and control, the very thing Whittier's poems had lacked. But his prose had not lacked this quality, or, in fact, a sense of the biting phrase; now his verse could absorb the virtues of his prose. It could learn, in addition to a sense of point, something of the poetic pungency of phrase and image, and the precision that sometimes marked the prose. He had referred to his poems as "fancies," and that is what they were, no more. Now he began to relate poetry, though blunderingly enough, to reality. And the process was slow. It was ten years — 1843 — before Whittier was able to write a piece as good as "Massachusetts to Virginia." It was effective propaganda; it had content and was organized to make a point. Here Whittier had at least avoided his besetting sin of wandering and padding, and we have only to set it in contrast to a piece like "The Panorama" (which actually was much later) to understand its virtues.

Whittier had to wait seven more years before, at the age of forty-two, he could write his first really fine poem. This piece, the famous "Ichabod," came more directly and personally out of his political commitment than any previous work. On March 7, 1850, Daniel Webster, senator from Massachusetts, spoke on behalf of the more stringent Fugitive Slave Bill that had just been introduced by Whittier's ex-idol Henry Clay; and the poem, which appeared shortly after in the *Na-*

tional Era of Washington, a paper of the "political" wing of the abolition movement,* laments the loss of the more recent and significant idol. "This poem," Whittier wrote later, "was the outcome of the surprise and grief and forecast of evil consequences which I felt on reading the seventh of March Speech by Daniel Webster. . . ." But here the poet remembers his poem, which does exploit dramatically surprise and grief, better than he remembers the facts of its origin; he could scarcely have felt literal surprise at Webster's speech, for as early as 1847, in a letter to Sumner, Whittier had called Webster a "colossal coward," because of his attitude toward the annexation of Texas and the Mexican war.

Here is the poem:

> So fallen! so lost! the light withdrawn
>   Which once he wore!
> The glory from his gray hairs gone
>   Forevermore!
>
> Revile him not, the Tempter hath
>   A snare for all;
> And pitying tears, not scorn and wrath,
>   Befit his fall!
>
> Oh, dumb be passion's stormy rage,
>   When he who might
> Have lighted up and led his age,
>   Falls back in night.
>
> Scorn! would the angels laugh, to mark
>   A bright soul driven,
> Fiend-goaded, down the endless dark,
>   From hope and heaven!
>
> Let not the land once proud of him
>   Insult him now,
> Nor brand with deeper shame his dim,
>   Dishonored brow.

* In which Whittier's only novel — or near-novel — *Margaret Smith's Journal*, had appeared the previous year, and in which *Uncle Tom's Cabin* was to appear.

But let its humbled sons, instead,
   From sea to lake,
A long lament, as for the dead,
   In sadness make.

Of all we loved and honored, naught
   Save power remains;
A fallen angel's pride of thought,
   Still strong in chains

All else is gone; from those great eyes
   The soul has fled:
When faith is lost, when honor dies,
   The man is dead!

Then, pay the reverence of old days
   To his dead fame;
Walk backward, with averted gaze,
   And hide the shame!

The effectiveness of "Ichabod," certainly one of the most telling poems of personal attack in English, is largely due to the subtlety of dramatization. At the center of the dramatization lies a division of feeling on the part of the poet; the poem is not a simple piece of vituperation, but represents a tension between old trust and new disappointment, old admiration and new rejection, the past and the present. The Biblical allusion in the title sets this up: "And she named the child Ichabod, saying, the glory is departed from Israel" (I Samuel, 4:21). The glory has departed, but grief rather than rage, respect for the man who was once the vessel of glory rather than contempt, pity for his frailty rather than condemnation — these are the emotions recommended as appropriate. We may note that not only are they appropriate as a generosity of attitude; they are also the emotions that are basically condescending, that put the holder of the emotions above the object of them, and that make the most destructive assault on the ego of the object. If Webster had been motivated by ambition, then pity is the one attitude his pride could not forgive.

27

The Biblical allusion at the end offers a brilliant and concrete summary of the complexity of feeling in the poem. As Notley Sinclair Maddox has pointed out (*Explicator*, April 1960), the last stanza is based on Genesis 9:20–25. Noah, in his old age, plants a vineyard, drinks the wine, and is found drunk and naked in his tent by his youngest son Ham, who merely reports the fact to his brothers Shem and Japheth. Out of filial piety, they go to cover Noah's shame, but "their faces were backward, and they saw not their father's nakedness." Ham, for having looked upon Noah's nakedness, is cursed as a "servant of servants" to his "brethren."

The allusion works as a complex and precise metaphor: The great Webster of the past, who, in the time of the debate with Robert Young Hayne (1830) had opposed the slave power and thus established his reputation, has now become obsessed with ambition (drunk with wine) and has exposed the nakedness of human pride and frailty. The conduct of Shem and Japheth sums up, of course, the attitude recommended by the poet. As an ironical adjunct, we may remember that the Biblical episode was used from many a pulpit as a theological defense of slavery, Ham, accursed as a "servant of servants," being, presumably, the forefather of the black race.

We may look back at the first stanza to see another complex and effective metaphor, suggested rather than presented. The light is withdrawn, and the light is identified, by the appositive construction, with the "glory" of Webster's gray hair — the glory being the achievement of age and the respect due to honorable age, but also the image of a literal light, an aureole about the head coming like a glow from the literal gray hair. This image fuses with that of the "fallen angel" of line 27 and the dimness of the "dim, dishonored brow" in lines 19 and 20. In other words, by suggestion, one of the things that holds the poem together (as contrasted with the logical sequence of the statement) is the image of the angel Lucifer, the light-bearer, fallen by excess of pride. Then in lines 29–30, the light image, introduced in the first stanza with the aureole about the gray hair, appears as an inward light shed outward, the "soul" that had once shone from Webster's eyes (he had remarkably large and lustrous dark eyes). But the soul is now dead, the light "withdrawn," and we have by suggestion a death's head with the eyes hollow and blank. How subtly the abstract ideas of "faith" and "honor" are drawn into this image, and how subtly the image itself is related to the continuing play of variations of the idea of light and dark.

From the point of view of technique this poem is, next to "Telling the Bees," Whittier's most perfectly controlled and subtle composition. This is true not only of the dramatic ordering and interplay of imagery, but also of the handling of rhythm as related to meter and stanza, and to the verbal texture. For Whittier, in those rare moments when he could shut out the inane gabble of the sweet singers, and of his own incorrigible meter-machine, could hear the true voice of feeling. But how rarely he heard — or trusted — the voice of feeling. He was, we may hazard, afraid of feeling. Unless, of course, a feeling had been properly disinfected.

In the "war with wrong," Whittier wrote a number of poems that were, in their moment, effectively composed, but only three, aside from "Ichabod," that survive to us as poetry. To one, "Song of Slaves in the Desert," we shall return, but the others too mark significant moments in Whittier's poetic development.

"The Panorama," of 1855, though it is diffuse and not well organized, has strokes of shrewd observation, accurate phrasing, and controlled irony. For instance, here is the village of the southern frontier, unkempt and slatternly, a combination of "vulgar newness" and "premature decay":

> A tavern, crazy with its whiskey brawls,
> With *"Slaves at Auction!"* garnishing its walls;
> Without, surrounded by a motley crowd,
> The shrewd-eyed salesman, garrulous and loud,

29

A squire or colonel in his pride of place,
Known at free fights, the caucus, and the race;
Prompt to proclaim his honor without blot,
And silence doubters with a ten-pace shot;
Mingling the negro-driving bully's rant
With pious phrase and democratic cant,
Yet never scrupling, with a filthy jest,
To sell the infant from its mother's breast,

The "Letter from a Missionary of the Methodist Episcopal Church South, in Kansas, to a Distinguished Politician," not only marks a high point in Whittier's poetic education but may enlighten us about the relation of that education to his activity as a journalist and propagandist. The poem, as the title indicates, grew out of the struggle between the pro-slavery and the free-state forces for the control of "Bleeding Kansas." Though the poem appeared in 1854, four years after "Ichabod," it shows us more clearly than the earlier piece how the realism, wit, and irony of Whittier's prose could be absorbed into a composition that is both tendentious and poetic. The tendentious element is converted into poetry by the force of its dramatization — as in the case of "Ichabod" — but here specifically by an ironic ventriloquism, the device of having the "Letter" come from the pen of the godly missionary:

Last week — the Lord be praised for all
     His mercies
To His unworthy servant! — I arrived
Safe at the Mission, *via* Westport; where
I tarried over night, to aid in forming
A Vigilance Committee, to send back,
In shirts of tar, and feather-doublets quilted
With forty stripes save one, all Yankee
     comers,
Uncircumcised and Gentile, aliens from
The Commonwealth of Israel, who despise
The prize of the high calling of the saints,
Who plant amidst this heathen wilderness
Pure gospel institutions, sanctified

By patriarchal use. The meeting opened
With prayer, as was most fitting. Half
    an hour,
Or thereaway, I groaned, and strove, and
    wrestled,
As Jacob did at Penuel, till the power
Fell on the people, and they cried "Amen!"
"Glory to God!" and stamped and clapped
    their hands;
And the rough river boatmen wiped their eyes;
"Go it, old hoss!" they cried, and cursed the
    niggers —
Fulfilling thus the word of prophecy,
"Cursed be Canaan."

By the ventriloquism the poem achieves a control of style, a fluctuating tension between the requirements of verse and those of "speech," a basis for the variations of tone that set up the sudden poetic, and ironic, effect at the end:

P.S. All's lost. Even while I write these
    lines,
The Yankee abolitionists are coming
Upon us like a flood — grim, stalwart men,
Each face set like a flint of Plymouth Rock
Against our institutions — staking out
Their farm lots on the wooded Wakarusa,
Or squatting by the mellow-bottomed Kansas;
The pioneers of mightier multitudes,
The small rain-patter, ere the thunder shower
Drowns the dry prairies. Hope from man is not.
Oh, for a quiet berth at Washington,
Snug naval chaplaincy, or clerkship, where
These rumors of free labor and free soil
Might never meet me more. Better to be
Door-keeper in the White House, than to dwell
Amidst these Yankee tents, that, whitening, show
On the green prairie like a fleet becalmed.
Methinks I hear a voice come up the river
From those far bayous, where the alligators
Mount guard around the camping filibusters:
"Shake off the dust of Kansas. Turn to Cuba

31

(That golden orange just about to fall,
O'er-ripe, into the Democratic lap;)
Keep pace with Providence, or, as we say,
Manifest destiny. Go forth and follow
The message of *our* gospel, thither borne
Upon the point of Quitman's bowie-knife,
And the persuasive lips of Colt's revolvers.
There may'st thou, underneath thy vine and
    fig-tree,
Watch thy increase of sugar cane and negroes,
Calm as a patriarch in his eastern tent!"
Amen: So mote it be. So prays your friend.

Here quite obviously the ventriloquism is what gives the poem a "voice," and the fact instructs us how Whittier, less obviously, develops through dramatization a voice in "Ichabod." The voice of a poem is effective — is resonant — insofar as it bespeaks a life behind that voice, implies a dramatic issue by which that life is defined. I have spoken of the complexity of feeling behind the voice of "Ichabod," and in the present case we find such a complexity in the character of the missionary himself. At first glance, we have the simple irony of the evil man cloaking himself in the language of the good. But another irony, and deeper, is implicit in the poem: the missionary may not be evil, after all; he may even be, in a sense, "good" — that is, be speaking in perfect sincerity, a man good but misguided; and thus we have the fundamental irony of the relation of evil and good in human character, action, and history. Whittier was a polemicist, and a very astute one, as the "Letter" in its primary irony exemplifies. But he was also a devout Quaker, and by fits and starts a poet, and his creed, like his art, would necessarily give a grounding for the secondary, and deeper, irony, an irony that implies humility and forgiveness.

❧ ☙

What I have been saying is that by repudiating poetry Whittier became a poet. His image of knocking Pegasus on the head tells a deeper truth than he knew; by getting rid of the "poetical" notion of poetry, he was able, eventually, to ground his poetry on experience. In the years of his crusade and of the Civil War, he was learning this, even though the process was, as I have said, slow. It was a process that seems to have been developed by fits and starts, trial and error, by floundering rather than by rational understanding. Whittier was without much natural taste and almost totally devoid of critical judgment, and he seems to have had only a flickering awareness of what he was doing — though he did have a deep awareness, it would seem, of his personal situation. As a poet he was trapped in the automatism and compulsiveness that, in "Amy Wentworth," he defined as the "automatic play of pen and pencil, solace to our pain" — the process that writing seems to have usually been for him. Even after a triumph, he could fall back into this dreary repetitiveness.

The mere mass of his published work in verse between 1843 and the Civil War indicates something of this undirected compulsiveness of composition that went on after he had decided to abandon poetry. In 1843 appeared *Lays of My Home*, in 1849 what amounted to a collected edition, in 1850 *Songs of Labor*, in 1853 *The Chapel of the Hermits and Other Poems*, in 1856 *The Panorama and Other Poems*, in 1857 the *Poetical Works*, in two volumes, and in 1860, *Home Ballads and Poems*. But in this massive and blundering production there had been a growth. In 1843 even poems like "To My Old Schoolmaster," "The Barefoot Boy," "Maud Muller," "Lines Suggested by Reading a State Paper," and "Kossuth" would have been impossible, not to mention "Skipper Ireson's Ride," which exhibits something of the élan of traditional balladry and something of the freedom of living language of "Ichabod" and the "Letter." But nothing short of a miracle, and a sudden miraculous understanding of Wordsworth and the traditional ballad, accounts for a little masterpiece like "Telling the Bees." There had been the technical development, but something else was happening too, something more difficult to define; Whittier was stumbling, now and then, on the subjects that might release the inner energy necessary for real poetry.

There was, almost certainly, a deep streak of grievance and undischarged anger in Whittier, for which the abolitionist poems (and editorials) could allow a hallowed — and disinfected — expression; simple indignation at fate could become "righteous indignation," and the biting sarcasm was redeemed by the very savagery of the bite. But there was another subject which released, and more deeply, the inner energy — the memory of the past, more specifically the childhood past, nostalgia, shall we say, for the happy, protected time before he knew the dark inward struggle, the outer struggle with "strong-willed men" (as he was to put it in "To My Sister") to which he had to steel himself, the collapses, and the grinding headaches. Almost everyone has an Eden time to look back on, even if it never existed and he has to create it for his own delusion; but for Whittier the need to dwell on this lost Eden was more marked than is ordinary. If the simple indignation against a fate that had deprived him of the security of childhood could be transmuted into righteous indignation, both forms of indignation could be redeemed in a dream of Eden innocence. This was the subject that could summon up Whittier's deepest feeling and release his fullest poetic power.

Furthermore, if we review the poems after 1850, we find a subsidiary and associated theme, sometimes in the same poem. In poems like "Maud Muller," "Kathleen," "Mary Garvin," "The Witch's Daughter," "The Truce of Piscataqua," "My Playmate," "The Countess," and "Telling the Bees," there is the theme of the lost girl, a child or a beloved, who may or may not be, in the course of a poem, recovered. Some of these poems, notably "Maud Muller" and "Kathleen," involve the question of differences of social rank, as does "The

34

Truce of Piscataqua" if we read blood for social difference, and "Marguerite" and "Mary Garvin" if we read the bar of religion in the same way. This last theme, in fact, often appears; we have it in "Amy Wentworth," "The Countess," and "Among the Hills," all of which belong to the mature period of Whittier's work, when he was looking nostalgically backward. But this theme of the lost girl, especially when the loss is caused by difference in social rank or the religious bar, even though it clearly repeats a theme enacted in Whittier's personal life, never really touched the spring of poetry in him except in "Telling the Bees," where it is crossed with the theme of childhood to mitigate the pang of the sexual overtones. The theme of the lost girl, taken alone, belonged too literally, perhaps, to the world of frustration. In life Whittier had worked out the problem and had survived by finding the right kind of action for himself, a "sanctified" action, and this action could, as we have seen, contribute to some of his best poetry; but more characteristically, his poetic powers were released by the refuge in assuagement, the flight into Eden, and this was at once his great limitation and the source of his fullest success.

For the poems specifically of nostalgia for childhood, we have "To My Old Schoolmaster," "The Barefoot Boy," "The Playmate," "The Prelude" (to "Among the Hills"), "To My Sister, with a copy of *The Supernaturalism of New England*," "In School-Days," "Telling the Bees," and preeminently *Snow-Bound*. It is not so much the number of poems involved that is significant, but the coherent quality of feeling and, by and large, the poetic quality in contrast to his other work. As Whittier puts it in "The Prelude," he was more and more impelled to

> . . . idly turn
> The leaves of memory's sketch-book, dreaming o'er
> Old summer pictures of the quiet hills,
> And human life, as quiet, at their feet.

He was, as he shrewdly saw himself in "Questions of Life," an "over-wearied child," seeking in "cool and shade his peace to find," in flight

> From vain philosophies, that try
> The sevenfold gates of mystery,
> And, baffled ever, babble still,
> Word-prodigal of fate and will;
> From Nature, and her mockery, Art,
> And book and speech of men apart,
> To the still witness in my heart.

As a young man hot with passion and ambition, and later as a journalist, agitator, and propagandist, he had struggled with the world, but there had always been the yearning for total peace which could be imaged in the Quaker meeting-house, but more deeply in childhood, as he summarized it in "To My Sister":

> And, knowing how my life hath been
> A weary work of tongue and pen,
> A long, harsh strife with strong-willed men,
>   Thou wilt not chide my turning
> To con, at times, an idle rhyme,
> To pluck a flower from childhood's clime,
> Or listen, at Life's noonday chime,
>   For the sweet bells of Morning!

The thing from which he fled but did not mention was, of course, inner struggle, more protracted and more bitter than the outer with "strong-willed men."

⤙ ৪⤚

"To My Old Schoolmaster," which appeared in 1851, just after Whittier's great poetic breakthrough with "Ichabod," is the germ of *Snow-Bound*, the summarizing poem of Whittier's basic impulse. It can be taken as such a germ not merely because it turns back to the early years, but because Joshua Coffin, the schoolmaster, was associated with certain events that we may regard as Whittier's rites of passages. It was Coffin who, when Whittier was a boy of fourteen, sat by the family fire and read aloud from Burns. It was Coffin who was with Whittier at the founding of the American Anti-Slavery Society in Philadelphia, in 1833. It was Coffin who early encouraged Whittier's historical and antiquarian interests (a fact that explains certain passages in the poem), and shared in his religious sense of the world; and in this last connection, it is logical to assume that when, late in life, Coffin, a sweet-natured and devout man, fell prey to the conviction that he was not among the "elect" and would be damned, the fact would stir the aging Whittier's deepest feelings about the meaning of his own experience. Be that as it may, when Coffin died, in June 1864, just before the death of Whittier's sister Elizabeth, which provoked *Snow-Bound*, Whittier felt, as he said in a letter, that he had lost "another of the old landmarks of the past." This bereavement would be absorbed into the more catastrophic one about to occur, just as the figure of Coffin would be absorbed into that of the schoolmaster in the poem that is ordinarily taken to refer, as we shall see, to a certain George Haskell.

Though "To My Old Schoolmaster" is a germ of *Snow-Bound*, an even earlier poem, "Song of Slaves in the Desert" of 1847, indicates more clearly the relation of the poems inspired by Whittier's "war on wrong" to the poems of personal inspiration. The "Song," the best poem done by Whittier up to that time, dramatizes the homesickness of the slaves, the theme of nostalgia, and since the slaves are, specifically, female, affords, too, the first example of the theme of the lost girl. The poem begins:

> Where are we going? where are we going,
>   Where are we going, Rubee?
>
> Lord of peoples, lord of lands,
> Look across these shining sands,
> Through the furnace of the noon,
> Through the white light of the moon.

> Strong the Ghiblee wind is blowing,
> Strange and large the world is growing!
> Speak and tell us where we are going,
>   Where are we going, Rubee? *

But "Ichabod," too, exhibits the theme of nostalgia, though in a somewhat more indirect and complex way. To begin with, the title declares that the theme is a lament for departed glory. Literally the glory is that of Webster, who has betrayed his trust, but also involved is the "glory" of those who trusted, who had trailed their own clouds of glory, not of strength and dedication, but of innocence, simplicity, and faith. The followers are, shall we say, children betrayed by their natural protector, for as the Biblical reference indicates, they are the sons of the drunken Noah. In the massiveness of the image, however, the father betrays the sons not only by wine but by death, for it is a death's head with empty eye-sockets that is the most striking fact of the poem. Here the evitable moral betrayal is equated, imagistically, with the inevitable and morally irrelevant fact of death. But by the same token, as a conversion of the proposition, the fact of death in the morally irrelevant course of nature is, too, a moral betrayal. The child, in other words, cannot forgive the course of nature — the fate — that leaves him defenseless.

* Whittier gives the following note on the poem from Richardson's *Journal in Africa*: "Sebah, Oasis of Fezzan, 10*th March*, 1846.— This evening the female slaves were unusually excited in singing, and I had the curiosity to ask my negro servant, Said, what they were singing about. As many of them were natives of his own country, he had no difficulty in translating the Mandara or Bornou language. I had often asked the Moors to translate their songs for me, but got no satisfactory account from them. Said at first said, 'Oh, they sing of *Rubee*' (God). 'What do you mean?' I replied, impatiently. 'Oh, don't you know?' he continued, 'they asked God to give them their *Atka*?' (certificate of freedom). I inquired, 'Is that all?' Said: 'No; they say, "Where are we going? The world is large. *O God! Where are we going? O God!*"' I inquired, 'What else?' Said: 'They remember their country, Bornou, and say, "*Bornou was a pleasant country, full of all good things; but this is a bad country, and we are miserable!*"' 'Do they say anything else?' Said: 'No; they repeat these words over and over again, and add, "O God! give us our *Atka, and let us return again to our dear home.*"'"

In connection with this purely latent content of the imagery, we may remark that Whittier, in looking back on the composition of the poem, claimed that he had recognized in Webster's act the "forecast of evil consequences" and knew the "horror of such a vision." For him this was the moment of confronting the grim actuality of life. It was, as it were, a political rite of passage. Here the protector has become the betrayer — has "died." So, in this recognition of the terrible isolation of maturity, "Ichabod," too, takes its place in the massive cluster of poems treating the nostalgia of childhood that prevision *Snow-Bound*.*

Let us glance at a later poem, "The Pipes at Lucknow: An Incident of the Sepoy Mutiny," that seems, at first glance, even more unrelated to the theme of childhood than does "Ichabod." But as "Ichabod" is associated with "To My Old Schoolmaster," a more explicit poem of childhood, so "Lucknow" is associated with "Telling the Bees." If we translate "Lucknow," we have something like this: The Scots have left home (i.e., have grown up) and are now beleaguered.

> Day by day the Indian tiger
> Louder yelled, and nearer crept;
> Round and round the jungle-serpent
> Near and nearer circles swept.

* "Ichabod" has thematic parallels with Hawthorne's great story "My Kinsman, Major Molineux." Both concern the degrading of a "father," Noah — as — Webster in his drunkenness and the Major at the hands of the mob. Both concern the son's involvement in the degrading: Whittier repudiates Webster even as Robin joins the mob in repudiating Molineux. Both works concern a betrayal by the father: Webster of his political trust, and Molineux, less precisely, in being an agent of the King and not of the colonists (i.e., children). Both concern what Hawthorne calls a majesty in ruins and in this connection involve deep ambivalences of the son toward the father. And in both, the son is thrown back upon his own resources, Whittier as is implied in his comment on the poem, and Robin quite specifically when he is offered the chance of going home or staying in Boston to "rise" by his own "efforts."

There is, probably, one great difference between the two works. It is hard not to believe that Hawthorne was conscious of what is at stake in his work, and it is hard to believe that Whittier was not unconscious of certain implications in "Ichabod."

The "Indian tiger" and the "jungle-serpent" are melodramatic versions of the "strong-willed men" and other manifestations of the adult world that Whittier had steeled himself to cope with, and from which he had turned, as the Scots turn now, on hearing the pipes, to seek assuagement in the vision of home. As another factor in this equation, we may recall that Whittier had early identified his father's rocky acres with the Scotland of Burns, and so the mystic "pipes o' Havelock" are the pipes of Haverhill.

With one difference: the pipes of Havelock announce not merely a vision of assuagement but also a vengeful carnage to be wrought on all those evil forces and persons that had robbed the child of "home," on the "strong-willed men" and the "Indian tiger" and the "jungle-serpent." Furthermore, since in the inner darkness, where their dramas are enacted, desire, fear, and hatred know no logic or justice beyond their own incorrigible natures, we may see distorted in the dark face of the "Indian tiger" and the "jungle-serpent" the the dark faces of those poor slaves in Dixie — for it was all their fault, they were the enemy, if it had not been for them Whittier would never have been drawn forth from the daydreams and neurotic indulgences of his youth into the broad daylight of mature and objective action.*

Whittier, it should be remembered, recognized in himself an appetite for violence. "I have still strong suspicions," he would write in one of his essays, "The Training," "that somewhat of the old Norman blood, something of the grim Berserker spirit, has been bequeathed to me." So, paradoxically, but in the deepest logic of his nature, this strain of violence is provoked against these forces that would threaten

* The poem may be taken as a kind of racist nightmare, like that of Isaac McCaslin in Faulkner's story "Delta Autumn," when he lies shaking with horror at his vision of the wilderness ruined to make room for a world of "usury and mortgage and bankruptcy and measureless wealth, Chinese and African and Aryan and Jew all breed, and spawn together until no man has time to say which one is which nor cares." Needless to say, Whittier's "nightmare," like Ike's, was conquered.

40

the "peace" of childhood, and it is by the gentle "air of Auld Lang Syne" rising above the "cruel roll of war-drums" that the vengeful slaughter is justified and the gentle Quaker poet breaks blamelessly out in warlike glee in such lines as

> And the tartan clove the turban
> As the Goomtee cleaves the plain.

"Lucknow," in fact, seems nearer to Kipling than to the saint of Amesbury, the abolitionist, and the libertarian poet who, in this very period, was writing poems deeply concerned with the freedom of Italians ("From Perugia," 1858, and "Italy," 1860) if not with that of Sepoys. But it is, as I have suggested, even nearer that gentle little masterpiece of nostalgia, "Telling the Bees." Both would seem to be conditioned by the same traumatic event, the death of Whittier's mother, which occurred in December 1857.

On February 16, 1858, Whittier sent "Telling the Bees" (originally called "The Bees of Fernside") to James Russell Lowell at the *Atlantic Monthly*, saying, "What I call simplicity may be only silliness." It was not silliness. It was a pure and beautiful little poem informed by the flood of feeling that broke forth at the death of the mother.

> Here is the place; right over the hill
>   Runs the path I took;
> You can see the gap in the old wall still,
>   And the stepping-stones in the shallow brook.
>
> There is the house, with the gate red-barred,
>   And the poplars tall;
> And the barn's brown length, and the cattle-yard,
>   And the white horns tossing above the wall.
>
> There are the beehives ranged in the sun;
>   And down by the brink
> Of the brook are her poor flowers, weed-o'errun,
>   Pansy and daffodil, rose and pink.
>
> A year has gone, as the tortoise goes,
>   Heavy and slow;

And the same rose blows, and the same sun glows,
  And the same brook sings of a year ago.

There's the same sweet clover-smell in the breeze;
  And the June sun warm
Tangles his wings of fire in the trees,
  Setting, as then, over Fernside farm.

I mind me how with a lover's care
  From my Sunday coat
I brushed off the burrs, and smoothed my hair,
  And cooled at the brookside my brow and throat.

Since we parted, a month had passed, —
  To love, a year;
Down through the beeches I looked at last
  On the little red gate and the well-sweep near.

I can see it all now, — the slantwise rain
  Of light through the leaves,
The sundown's blaze on her window-pane,
  The bloom of her roses under the eaves.

Just the same as a month before, —
  The house and the trees,
The barn's brown gable, the vine by the door, —
  Nothing changed but the hives of bees.

Before them, under the garden wall,
  Forward and back,
Went drearily singing the chore-girl small,
  Draping each hive with a shred of black.

Trembling, I listened: the summer sun
  Had the chill of snow;
For I knew she was telling the bees of one
  Gone on the journey we all must go!

Then I said to myself, "My Mary weeps
  For the dead to-day:
Haply her blind old grandsire sleeps
  The fret and the pain of his age away."

But her dog whined low; on the doorway sill,
  With his cane to his chin,
The old man sat; and the chore-girl still
  Sung to the bees stealing out and in.

And the song she was singing ever since
   In my ear sounds on: —
"Stay at home, pretty bees, fly not hence!
Mistress Mary is dead and gone!"

The setting of the poem is a scrupulous re-creation of the farmstead where Whittier spent his youth, as Samuel T. Pickard, in his *Life and Letters of Whittier*, reports in 1894:

There were beehives on the garden terrace near the well-sweep, occupied, perhaps, by the descendants of Thomas Whittier's bees. The approach to the house from over the northern shoulder of Job's Hill by a path that was in constant use in his boyhood, and is still in existence, is accurately described in the poem. The "gap in the old wall" is still to be seen, and "the stepping-stones in the shallow brook" are still in use. His sister's garden was down by the brookside in front of the house, and her daffodils are perpetuated, and may now be found in their season each year in that place. The red-barred gate, the poplars, the cattle-yard with "the white horns tossing over the wall," — these were all part of Whittier's boy life on the old farm. Even the touch of "the sundown's blaze on her window-pane" is realistic. The only place from which the blaze of the setting sun could be seen reflected in the windows of the old mansion was from the path so perfectly described, and no doubt the poet had often noticed the phenomenon in his youth while approaching the house in this direction.

The poem was composed almost thirty years after Whittier had gone out into the world, and some twenty-two years after he had sold the home place and moved the family to Amesbury. Not only the same nostalgia that informs *Snow-Bound* is part of the motivation of this poem, but also the same literalism. But more than mere literalism seems to be involved in the strange fact that Whittier keeps his sister Mary — or at least her name — in the poem, and keeps her there to kill her off; and there is, of course, the strange fact that he cast a shadowy self — the "I" of the poem — in the role of the lover of Mary, again playing here with the theme of lost love, of the lost girl, but bringing the story within the family circle, curiously

43

coalescing the youthful yearning for sexual love and the childhood yearning for love and security within the family circle. And all this at a time when Mary was very much alive.

◆

Just as the shock of his mother's death turned Whittier's imagination back to the boyhood home and presumably released the energy for "Telling the Bees," so the death of his sister Elizabeth lies behind *Snow-Bound*. The relation of Whittier to this sister, who shared his literary and other tastes, who herself wrote verses (often indistinguishable in their lack of distinction from the mass of her brother's work), who was a spirited and humorous person, and who, as a spinster, was a companion to his bachelorhood, was of a more complex and intimate kind than even that of Whittier to his mother. She was, as Lucy Larcom,* a poetess of some small fame, observed in her diary, "dear Lizzy, his sole home-flower, the meek lily-blossom that cheers and beautifies his life"; and when she died, on September 3, 1864, Whittier said "the great motive of my life seems lost."

Shortly before Elizabeth's death there had been another crisis in Whittier's life, the end of his second and final romance with Elizabeth Lloyd, whom I have already mentioned. The relation with her was not merely another of his frustrated romances. He had known her for some twenty-five years, from the time when he was thirty. She was good-looking, wrote verses, painted pictures, believed ardently in abolition, and was a Quaker to boot. What could have been more appropriate? She even fell in love with him, if we can judge from the appeals in letters written toward the end of her first connection with him: "Spirit, silent, dumb and cold! What hath possessed thee?" Or: "Do come, Greenleaf! I am almost forgetting how thee looks and seems." But Greenleaf was beating one of his strategic retreats; so she cut her losses, got to

* Lucy Larcom was, apparently, also one of the ladies who were in love, to no avail, with the poet.

work and made a literary reputation of sorts, married a non-Quaker and got "read out of meeting."

After her husband's death, however, Elizabeth Lloyd, now Howell, reappeared in Whittier's life. They became constant companions. Both suffered from severe headaches, but they found that if they caressed each other's hair and massaged each other's brows, the headaches would go away. Or at least Whittier's headache would, and he proposed to her. She refused him, but not definitively, and the dalliance went on. Even a quarrel about Quakerism did not end it. In any case, it did end, and in later years the lady nursed a grievance and spoke bitterly of the old sweetheart.

Whittier had scarcely escaped from Elizabeth Howell's healing hands when his sister Elizabeth died. If he still clung to the explanation that his long bachelorhood had been due to "the care of an aged mother, and the duty owed a sister in delicate health," its last vestige of plausibility was now removed. He was now truly alone, with no landmarks left from the Edenic past. There was only memory.

~§ ξ~

Before the end of the month in which Elizabeth died, Whittier sent to the *Atlantic* a poem which he said had "beguiled some weary hours." It was "The Vanishers," based on a legend he had read in Schoolcraft's famous *History, Condition, and Prospects of the American Indians*, about the beautiful spirits who fleetingly appear to beckon the living on to what Whittier calls "The Sunset of the Blest." To the Vanishers, Whittier likens the beloved dead:

> Gentle eyes we closed below,
>   Tender voices heard once more,
> Smile and call us, as they go
>   On and onward, still before.

The poem is, in its basic impulse, the first draft of *Snow-Bound*.

In a very special way *Snow-Bound* summarizes Whittier's life and work. We have already noted the obsessive theme of childhood nostalgia that leads to *Snow-Bound*, but as early as 1830, in "The Frost Spirit," we find the key situation of the family gathered about a fire while the "evil power" of the winter storm (and of the world) goes shrieking by. Whittier, too, had long been fumbling toward his great question of how to find in the contemplation of the past a meaning for the future. In "My Soul and I," of 1847, the soul that turns in fear from the unknown future to seek comfort in the "Known and Gone" must learn that "The past and the time to be are one,/And both are now."

The same issue reappears in "The Garrison of Cape Ann":

> The great eventful Present hides the Past; but
>   through the din
> Of its loud life hints and echoes from the life
>   behind steal in;
> And the lore of home and fireside, and the
>   legendary rhyme,
> Make the task of duty lighter which the true man
>   owes his time.

And it appears again in "The Prophecy of Samuel Sewall," of 1859.

As for the relation to the poet's personal life, *Snow-Bound* came not only after another manifestation of the old inhibition that forbade his seeking solace from Elizabeth Lloyd's healing hands — and this as he neared the age of sixty when the repudiation of the solace must have seemed catastrophically final; and not only after the death of the sister had deprived him of his "life-motive." It came, too, toward the end of the Civil War, when he could foresee the victory of the cause to which he had given his energies for more than thirty years and which had, in a sense, served as his justification for life and as a substitute for other aspects of life. Now the joy of victory would, necessarily, carry with it a sense of emptiness.

Furthermore, the victory itself was in terms sadly different, as Whittier recognized, from those that he had dreamed.

If *Snow-Bound* is, then, a summarizing poem for Whittier, it came, also, at a summarizing moment for the country. It came when the country — at least, the North — was poised on the threshold of a new life, the world of technology, big industry, big business, finance capitalism, and urban values; and at that moment, caught up in the promises of the future, the new breed of American could afford to look back on their innocent beginnings. The new breed could afford to pay for the indulgence of nostalgia; in fact, in the new affluence, they paid quite well for it. The book appeared on February 17, 1866,* and the success was immediate. For instance, in April, J. T. Fields, the publisher, wrote Whittier: "We can't keep the plaguey thing quiet. It goes and goes, and now, today, we are bankrupt again, not a one being in crib." The first edition earned Whittier $10,000 — a sum to be multiplied many times over if translated into present values. The poor man was, overnight, modestly rich.

The scene of the poem, the "Flemish picture" as Whittier calls it, the modest genre piece, is rendered with precise and loving care, and this had its simple nostalgic appeal for the generation who had come to town and made it, and a somewhat different appeal, compensatory and comforting, no doubt, for the generation that had stayed in the country and had not made it. But the poem is not simple, and it is likely that the appeals would have been far less strong and permanent if Whittier had not set the "idyl" in certain "perspectives" of deeper interpretation. In other words, it can be said of this poem, as of most poetry, that the effect does not depend so much on the thing looked at as on the way of the

---

* Melville's book of poems on the Civil War, *Battle-Pieces*, appeared almost simultaneously, and was a crashing failure. As *Snow-Bound* seemed to dwell merely on the simplicity of the past, *Battle-Pieces* analyzed some of the painful complexities of the war and the present, and recognized some of the painful paradoxes in the glowing promises of the future: not what the public wanted to hear.

looking. True, if there is nothing to look at, there can be no looking, but the way of the looking determines the kind of feeling that fuses with the object looked at.

Before we speak of the particular "perspectives" in which the poem is set, we may say that there is a preliminary and general one. This general perspective, specified in Whittier's dedicatory note to his "Winter Idyl," * denies that the poem is a mere "poem." The poem, that is, is offered as autobiography, with all the validation of fact. In other words, the impulse that had appeared in "The Vanishers" as fanciful is here given a grounding in the real world, and in presenting that world the poem explores a complex idea, how different from the vague emotion of "The Vanishers," concerning the human relation to Time.

The reality of that literal world is most obviously certified by the lovingly and precisely observed details: the faces

---

* Here is the beginning of the preparatory note: "The inmates of the family at the Whittier homestead who are referred to in the poem were my father, mother, my brother and two sisters, and my uncle and aunt both unmarried. In addition, there was the district school-master who boarded with us. The 'not unfeared, half-welcome guest' was Harriet Livermore, daughter of Judge Livermore, of New Hampshire, a young woman of fine natural ability, enthusiastic, eccentric, with slight control over her violent temper, which sometimes made her religious profession doubtful. She was equally ready to exhort in school-house prayer-meetings and dance in a Washington ball-room, while her father was a member of Congress. She early embraced the doctrine of the Second Advent, and felt it her duty to proclaim the Lord's speedy coming. With this message she crossed the Atlantic and spent the greater part of a long life in travelling over Europe and Asia. She lived some time with Lady Hester Stanhope, a woman as fantastic and mentally strained as herself, on the slope of Mt. Lebanon, but finally quarrelled with her in regard to two white horses with red marks on their backs which suggested the idea of saddles, on which her titled hostess expected to ride into Jerusalem with the Lord. A friend of mine found her, when quite an old woman, wandering in Syria with a tribe of Arabs, who with the Oriental notion that madness is inspiration, accepted her as their prophetess and leader. At the time referred to in *Snow-Bound* she was boarding at the Rocks Village about two miles from us."

Elsewhere, in a preparatory note to another poem, "The Countess," Whittier identifies the "wise old doctor" of *Snow-Bound* as Dr. Elias Weld of Haverhill, "the one cultivated man in the neighborhood," who had given the boy the use of his library.

48

sharpened by cold, the "clashing horn on horn" of the restless cattle in the barn, the "grizzled squirrel" dropping his
shell, the "board nails snapping in the frost" at night. This
general base of the style is low, depending on precision of
rendering rather than on the shock and brilliance of language
or image; but from this base certain positive poetic effects
emerge as accents and point of focus. For instance:

> A chill no coat, however stout,
> Of homespun stuff could quite shut out,
> A hard, dull bitterness of cold,
> That checked, mid-vein, the circling race
> Of life-blood in the sharpened face,
> The coming of the snow-storm told.
> The wind blew east; we heard the roar
> Of Ocean on his wintry shore,
> And felt the strong pulse throbbing there
> Beat with low rhythm our inland air.

Associated with this background realism of the style of the
poem we find a firm realism in the drawing of character.
Three of the portraits are sharp and memorable, accented
against the other members of the group and at the same time
bearing thematic relations to them: the spinster aunt, the
schoolmaster, and Harriet Livermore.

The aunt, who had a tragic love affair but who, as the
poem states, has found reconciliation with life, bears a
thematic relation to both Elizabeth Whittier and Whittier
himself. The schoolmaster, whose name Whittier could not
remember until near the end of his life, was a George Haskell,
who later became a doctor, practiced in Illinois and New
Jersey, and died in 1876 without even knowing, presumably,
of his role in the poem; but as I have pointed out, there are
echoes here, too, of Joshua Coffin. As for Harriet Livermore,
Whittier's note identifies her. The fact that the "warm, dark
languish of her eyes" might change to rage is amply docu-
mented by the fact that at one time, before the scene of *Snow-
Bound*, she had been converted to Quakerism, but during an

argument with another Quaker on a point of doctrine asserted her theological view by seizing a length of stove wood and laying out her antagonist. This, of course, ended her connection with the sect. In her restless search for a satisfying religion, she represents one strain of thought in nineteenth-century America, and has specific resemblances to the characters Nathan and Nehemiah in Melville's *Clarel*. As a "woman tropical, intense," and at the same time concerned with ideas and beliefs, she is of the type of Margaret Fuller, the model for Zenobia in the *Blithedale Romance* of Hawthorne.

To return to the structure of the poem, there are three particular "perspectives" — ways in which the material is to be viewed — that can be localized in the body of the work. These perspectives operate as inserts that indicate the stages of the dialectic of this poem. The first appears in lines 175 to 211, the second in lines 400 to 437, and the third in lines 715 to the end.

The first section of the poem (up to the first perspective) presents a generalized setting, the coming of the storm, the first night, the first day, and the second night. Here the outside world is given full value in contrast to the interior, especially in the following passage, which is set between two close-ups of the hearthside, that Eden spot surrounded by the dark world:

> The moon above the eastern wood
> Shown at its full; the hill-range stood
> Transfigured in the silver flood,
> Its blown snows flashing cold and keen,
> Dead white, save where some sharp ravine
> Took shadow, or the sombre green
> Of hemlocks turned to pitchy black
> Against the whiteness at their back.
> For such a world and such a night
> Most fitting that unwarming light,
> Which only seemed where'er it fell
> To make the coldness visible.

The setting, as I have said, is generalized; the individual characters have not yet emerged, the father having appeared in only one line of description and as a voice ordering the boys (John and his only brother Matthew) to dig a path, with the group at the fireside only an undifferentiated "we" (line 156). This section ends with the sharp focus on the mug of cider simmering between the feet of the andirons and the apples sputtering — the literal fire, the literal comfort against the threat of literal darkness and cold outside.

Now, with line 175, the first perspective is introduced:

> What matter how the night behaved?
> What matter how the north-wind raved?
> Blow high, blow low, not all its snow
> Could quench our hearth-fire's ruddy glow.

But immediately, even as he affirms the inviolability of the fireside world, the poet cries out:

> O Time and Change! — with hair as gray
> As was my sire's that winter day,
> How strange it seems, with so much gone
> Of life and love, to still live on!

From this remembered scene by the fireside only two of the participants survive, the poet and his brother (Matthew), who are now as gray as the father at that snowfall of long ago; for all are caught in Time, in this less beneficent snowfall that whitens every head, as the implied image seems to say. Given this process of the repetition of the life pattern of Time and Change, what, the poet asks, can survive? The answer is that "Love can never lose its own."

After the first perspective has thus developed a new meaning from the scene of simple nostalgia by the fire, the poem becomes a gallery of individual portraits, the father, the mother, the uncle, the aunt, the elder sister (Mary), and the younger (Elizabeth), the schoolmaster, and Harriet Livermore. That is, each individual brings into the poem a specific dramatization of the problem of Time. In the simplest di-

51

mension, they offer continuity and repetition: they, the old, were once young, and now sitting by the fire, with the young, tell of youth remembered against the background of age. More specifically, each of the old has had to try to come to terms with Time, and each portrait involves an aspect of the problem.

When the family portraits have been completed, the second perspective is introduced; this is concerned primarily with the recent bereavement, with the absent Elizabeth, and with the poet's personal future as he walks toward the night and sees (as an echo from "The Vanishers") Elizabeth's beckoning hand. Thus out of the theme of Time and Change emerges the theme of the Future, which is to be developed in the portraits of the schoolmaster and Harriet Livermore.

The first will make his peace in Time, by identifying himself with progressive social good (which, as a matter of fact, George Haskell had done by 1866). Harriet Livermore, though seeking, by her theological questing, a peace out of Time, has found no peace in Time, presumably because she cannot seek in the right spirit; with the "love within her mute" she cannot identify herself with the real needs of the world about her (as Aunt Mercy can and George Haskell will); she is caught in the "tangled skein of will and fate," and can only hope for a peace in Divine forgiveness, out of Time. After the portrait of Harriet Livermore, we find the contrast in the mother's attitude at the good-night scene: unlike Harriet she finds peace in the here-and-now, "food and shelter, warmth and health" and love, with no "vain prayers" but a willingness to act practically in the world — an idea that echoes the theme of "My Soul and I," already mentioned. And this is followed with the peace of night and the "reconciled" dream of summer in the middle of the winter, an image of both past and future in the turn of time.

With dawn, the present — not the past, not the future — appears, with its obligations, joys, and promises. Here there is a lag in the structure of the poem. When the snowbound

52

ones awake to the sound of "merry voices high and clear," the poem should, logically, move toward its fulfillment. But instead, after the active intrusion of the world and the present, we have the section beginning "So days went on" (line 674), and then the dead "filler" for some twenty lines. Whittier's literalism, his fidelity to irrelevant fact rather than to relevant meaning and appropriate structure of the whole, here almost destroy both the emotional and the thematic thrust, and it is due only to the power of the last movement that the poem is not irretrievably damaged.*

The third "perspective" (lines 715–59), which ends the poem, is introduced by these eloquent lines:

> Clasp, Angel of the backward look
> And folded wings of ashen gray
> And voice of echoes far away,
> The brazen covers of thy book;

Then follow certain new considerations. What is the relation between the dream of the past and the obligations and actions of the future? The answer is, of course, in the sense of continuity of human experience, found when one stretches the "hands of memory" to the "wood-fire's blaze" of the past; it is thus that one may discover the meaningfulness of obligation and action in Time, even as he discovers, in the specific memories of the past, an image for the values out of Time. The "idyl" is more than a "Flemish picture"; it is an image, and a dialectic, of one of life's most fundamental questions that is summed up in the haunting simplicity of the end:

> Sit with me by the homestead hearth,
> And stretch the hands of memory forth
> To warm them at the wood-fire's blaze!

---

* There are, in fact, other lags and fillers in the poem. For instance, there are repetitions in the two barn scenes (lines 21–30 and 81–92); it "happened" this way, so back we go to the barn for the retake. There are patches, too, where the mason piling bricks takes over from the poet, with monotonous versification; for instance, in lines 263–275, where the metrical pattern and the line stop the vital movement.

And thanks untraced to lips unknown
Shall greet me like the odors blown
From unseen meadows newly mown,
Or lilies floating in some pond,
Wood-fringed, the wayside gaze beyond;
The traveller owns the grateful sense
Of sweetness near, he knows not whence,
And, pausing, takes with forehead bare
The benediction of the air.

As a corollary to the third "perspective" generally considered, Whittier has, however, ventured a specific application. He refers not merely to the action in the future, in general, in relation to the past, but also, quite clearly, to the Civil War and the new order with its "larger hopes and graver fears" — the new order of "throngful city ways" as contrasted with the old agrarian way of life and thought. He invites the "worldling" — the man who, irreligiously, would see no meaning in the shared experience of human history, which to Whittier would have been a form of revelation — to seek in the past not only a sense of personal renewal and continuity, but also a sense of the continuity of the new order with the American past. This idea is clearly related to Whittier's conviction, already mentioned, that the course of development for America should be the fulfilling of the "implied intent" of the Constitution in particular, of the American revelation in general, and of God's will. And we may add that Whittier, by this, also gives another "perspective" in which his poem is to be read.

❧ ☙

If we leave *Snow-Bound*, the poem, and go back again to its springs in Whittier's personal story, we may find that it recapitulates in a new form an old issue. The story of his youth is one of entrapments — and of his failure to break out into the world of mature action. In love, politics, and poetry, he was constantly being involved in a deep, inner struggle, with the self-pity, the outrage, the headaches, the breakdowns. He was, to no avail, trying to break out of the "past" of childhood into the "future" of manhood — to achieve, in other words, a self.

The mad ambition that drove him to try to break out of the entrapments, became, in itself, paradoxically, another entrapment — another dead hand of the past laid on him. He cried out, "now, now!" — not even knowing what he cried out for, from what need for what reality. But nothing worked out, not love, or politics, or even poetry, that common substitute for success of a more immediate order. In poetry, in fact, he could only pile up words as a mason piles up bricks; he could only repeat, compulsively, the dreary clichés; his meter-making machine ground on, and nothing that came out was, he knew, real: his poems were only "fancies," as he called them, only an echo of the past, not his own present. And if he set out with the declared intention of being the poet of New England, his sense of its history was mere antiquarianism, mere quaintness: no sense of an abiding human reality. Again he was trapped in the past. All his passions strove, as he put it, "in chains." He found release from what he called "the pain of disappointment and the temptation to envy" only in repudiating the self, and all the self stood for, in order to save the self. He could find a cause that, because it had absorbed, shall we hazard, all the inner forces of the "past" that had thwarted his desires, could free him into some "future" of action.

So much for the story of the young Whittier.

But what of the old?

He had, in the end, fallen into another entrapment of the past. All action — and the possibility of continuing life — had been withdrawn: the solacing hands of Elizabeth Lloyd, the "great motive of . . . life" that the other Elizabeth represented, old friends such as Joshua Coffin, even the "cause" to which he had given his life and which had given his life meaning. Only memory — the past — was left. To live — to have a future — he had to re-fight the old battle of his youth on a new and more difficult terrain. He had to find a new way to make the past nourish the future.

It could not be the old way. The old way had been, in a sense, merely a surrender. By it, Whittier had indeed found a future, a life of action. But the victory had been incomplete, and the costs great; for we must remember that the grinding headaches continued and that the solacing hands of Elizabeth Lloyd had been, in the end, impossible for him.

The new way was more radical. That is, Whittier undertook to see the problem of the past and future as generalized rather than personal, as an issue confronting America, not only himself: furthermore, to see it *sub specie aeternitatis*, as an aspect of man's fate. And he came to see that man's fate is that he must learn to accept and use his past completely, knowingly, rather than to permit himself to be used, ignorantly, by it.

•❧ ❧•

Having struggled for years with the deep difficulties of his own life, Whittier at last found a way to fruitfully regard them, and *Snow-Bound* is the monument of this personal victory. No, it may be the dynamic image of the very process by which the victory itself was achieved. But there is another way in which we may regard it. It sets Whittier into relation to an obsessive and continuing theme in our literature, a theme that most powerfully appears in Cooper, Hawthorne, Melville, and Faulkner: what does the past mean to an American?

The underlying question is, of course, why a sense of the past should be necessary at all. Why in a country that was new — was all "future" — should the question have arisen at all? Cooper dealt with it in various dramatizations, most obviously in the figures of Hurry Harry and the old pirate in *Deerslayer* and that of the squatter in *The Prairie*, who are looters, exploiters, and spoilers of man and nature: none of these men has a sense of the pride and humility that history may inculcate. How close are these figures to those of Faulkner's world who have no past, or who would repudiate the past, who are outside history — for example, the Snopeses (descendants of bushwhackers who had no "side" in the Civil War), Popeye of *Sanctuary*, Jason and the girl Quentin of *The Sound and the Fury* (who repudiate the family and the past), and of course poor Joe Christmas of *Light in August*, whose story is the pathetic struggle of a man who, literally, has no past, who does not know who he is or his own reality. Whittier, too, understood the fate of the man who has no past — or who repudiates his past. This is his "worldling" of *Snow-Bound* (whom we may also take as an image of what the past might have been had the vainglorious dreams of his youth been realized), whom he calls to spread his hands before the warmth of the past in order to understand his own humanity, to catch the sweetness coming "he knows not where," and the "benediction of the air."

But, on the other side of this question, Whittier understood all too well the danger of misinterpreting the past — in his own case the danger of using the past as a refuge from reality. Faulkner, too, fully understood this particular danger and dramatized it early in *Sartoris* and later in "The Odor of Verbena." But the theme appears more strikingly and deeply philosophized in characters like Quentin Compson in *The Sound and the Fury* and Hightower in *Light in August*. But Faulkner understood other kinds of dangers of misinterpretation. Sutpen, with his "design" and no comprehension of the inwardness of the past, suggests, in spite of all differences, a parallel with Cooper's squatter in *The Prairie*, whose only link with the past is some tattered pages from the Old Testament that serve, in the end, to justify his killing of the brother-in-law (the pages having no word of the peace and brotherhood of the New Testament). But Faulkner's most complex instance of the misinterpretation of the past occurs with Ike McCaslin, who, horrified by the family crime of slavery and incest, thinks he can buy out simply by refusing to accept his patrimony: he does not realize that a true understanding of the past involves both an acceptance and a transcendence of the acceptance.

If we turn to Melville, we find in *Pierre, or the Ambiguities* the story of a man trapped, as Whittier was, in the past and desperately trying to free himself for adult action, just as we find in *Battle-Pieces*, in more general terms, the over-arching theme of the irony of history set against man's need to validate his life in action. And, for a variation on the general question, in *Clarel* we find the hero (who has no "past"— who is fatherless and has lost his God, and who does not know mother or sister) seeking in history a meaning of life, this quest occurring in the Holy Land, the birthplace of the spiritual history of the Western world; and it is significant that Clarel finds his only answer in the realization that men are "cross-bearers all" — that is, by identifying himself with the human community, in its fate of expiatory suffering — an answer very similar, though in a different tonality, to that of *Snow-Bound*.

With Hawthorne the same basic question is somewhat differently framed. We do not find figures with roles like those of Hurry Harry, the squatter, Joe Christmas, Hightower, or Clarel, but find, rather, a general approach to the meaning of the past embodied in Hawthorne's treatment of the history of New England. Nothing could be further than his impulse from the antiquarian and sentimental attitude of Whittier in his historical pieces or that of Longfellow. What Hawthorne found in the past was not the quaint charm of distance but the living issues of moral and psychological definition. What the fact of the past gave him was a distancing of the subject to gain an archetypal clarity and a mythic force. The sentimental flight into an assuagement possible in the past was the last thing he sought. He could praise the ancestors, but at the same time thank God for every year that had come to give distance from them. In his great novel and the tales the underlying theme concerns "legend" as contrasted with "action," the "past" as contrasted with the "future," as in the works of Cooper, Melville, and Faulkner; and sometimes, most obviously in "My Kinsman, Major Molineux," with this theme is intertwined the psychological struggle to achieve maturity, with the struggle seen as a "fate."

Whittier, though without the scale and power of Cooper, Hawthorne, Melville, and Faulkner, and though he was singularly lacking in their sense of historical and philosophic irony, yet shared their deep intuition of what it meant to be an American. Further, he shared their intuitive capacity to see personal fate as an image for a general cultural and philosophic situation. His star belongs in their constellation. If it is less commanding than any of theirs, it yet shines with a clear and authentic light.

❧

Whittier lived some twenty-five years after *Snow-Bound* and wrote voluminously. But, as always, the flashes of poetry were intermittent: "Abraham Davenport," "The Prelude," "The Hive at Gettysburg," "The Pressed Gentian," "At Last," and "To Oliver Wendell Holmes." To these might be added the elegy on Conductor Bradley ("A railway conductor who lost his life in an accident on a Connecticut railway, May 9, 1873"), which may claim immortality of a sort scarcely intended by the poet — as a work of grotesque humor and unconscious parody and self-parody. The world would be poorer without this accidental triumph of what we may call inspired bathos. The opening stanzas run:

> Conductor Bradley, (always may his name
> Be said with reverence!) as the swift
>   doom came,
> Smitten to death, a crushed and mangled frame,

Sank, with the brake he grasped just where
    he stood
To do the utmost that a brave man could,
And die, if needful, as a true man should.

Men stooped above him; women dropped their tears
On that poor wreck beyond all hopes or fears,
Lost in the strength and glory of his years.

What heard they? Lo! the ghastly lips of pain,
Dead to all thought save duty's, moved again;
"Put out the signals for the other train!"

Whittier had lived into a world totally strange to him. The world of industrialism and finance capitalism, of strikes and strikebreaking, meant no more to him than it would have to Emerson. While a man like William Dean Howells saw the Haymarket case as a crucial test of justice, Whittier simply could not understand the issue. But his fame was world-wide: the abolitionist, the hero, the humorist (for he was that, too, in his way), and to top it all, a sort of minor saint in outmoded Quaker dress. The house at Amesbury had long since become a point of pilgrimage, and many of the pilgrims were female, and often marriageable, or fancied themselves so. In Whittier's continuing bachelorhood, with a series of female friends and admirers, there ran a strain of flirtatiousness that more than one lady seems to have taken too seriously. The old fierce ambition had now shrunk to a small vanity that gratified itself in an excessive number of sittings for photographs and some devious tricks of self-advertisement, such as writing an interview with himself and disguising the identity of the interviewer, or doing the laudatory entry under his name in an encyclopedia of biography. So, too, the old passion that had striven "in chains" now flickered on in these little erotic charades. His ego needed these things even at the time when he had long since won the real battle against himself and fate, and even now when he could, without blame, turn his feelings and imagination to the safe past of the child by the fireside. Or perhaps now, as age drew on,

60

even with all of his humor, self-humor, self-knowledge, self-discipline, and real humility, he needed these old charades more than ever.

❦

Whittier died September 7, 1892, after a brief period of illness and a paralytic stroke. Toward the end, he was often heard to murmur, "Love — love to all the world." As he was dying, one of his relatives present by the bedside quoted his poem "At Last." He was buried in the section of the cemetery at Amesbury reserved for Friends. The grave was lined with fern and goldenrod, and the coffin was lowered to rest on a bed of roses. Nearby were the graves of the members of the family who had sat at the fireside of *Snow-Bound*.

❦

Whittier, as Van Wyck Brooks has observed, liked to turn an honest penny, and quietly, without anyone's being aware of it, he had turned a good many in his late years. He left an estate of $130,000. Among his bequests was a substantial one to the Hampton Institute, a school for Negroes and Indians, in Virginia. One of Whittier's last poems, "On the Big Horn," celebrates the fact that Chief Rain-in-the-Face, notable in the battle that ended Custer's career, had repented his old savage ways and applied to be admitted to the Institute "to know as the white men know."

SUGGESTED READINGS

Arms, George. *The Fields Were Green: A New View of Bryant, Whittier, Holmes, Lowell, and Longfellow.* Stanford, Calif.: Stanford University Press, 1953.

Bennett, Whitman. *Whittier: Bard of Freedom.* Chapel Hill: University of North Carolina Press, 1941.

Currier, Thomas Franklin, ed., *Elizabeth Lloyd and the Whittiers: A Budget of Letters.* Cambridge, Mass.: Harvard University Press, 1939.

Foerster, Norman. *Nature in American Literature.* New York: Macmillan, 1923.

Hall, Donald. "Whittier," *Texas Quarterly*, 3:165–174 (Autumn 1960).

Jones, Howard Mumford. "Whittier Reconsidered," *Essex Institute Historical Collections*, 93:231–246 (October 1957).

Leary, Lewis. *John Greenleaf Whittier.* New York: Twayne, 1961.

Miller, Perry. "John Greenleaf Whittier: The Conscience in Poetry," *Harvard Review*, 2:8–24 (1964).

Mordell, Albert. *Quaker Militant: John Greenleaf Whittier.* Boston: Houghton Mifflin, 1933.

More, Paul Elmer. *Shelburne Essays*, Third Series. New York: G. P. Putnam's Sons, 1907.

Pickard, John B. "Imagistic and Structural Unity in *Snow-Bound*," *College English*, 21:338–342 (March 1960).

———. *John Greenleaf Whittier: An Introduction and Interpretation.* New York: Barnes and Noble, 1961.

Pickard, Samuel T. *Life and Letters of John Greenleaf Whittier.* 2 vols. Boston: Houghton Mifflin, 1894.

———. *Whittier-Land: A Handbook of North Essex.* Boston: Houghton Mifflin, 1906.

Pollard, John A. *John Greenleaf Whitter: Friend of Man.* Boston: Houghton Mifflin, 1949.

Scott, Winfield Townley. "Poetry in America: A New Consideration of Whittier's Verse," *New England Quarterly*, 7:258–275 (June 1934).

Wagenknecht, Edward. *John Greenleaf Whittier: A Portrait in Paradox.* New York: Oxford University Press, 1967.

Waggoner, Hyatt. "What I Had I Gave: Another Look at Whittier," *Essex Institute Historical Collections*, 95:32–40 (January 1959).

Whittier, John Greenleaf. *The Writings of John Greenleaf Whittier*, ed. Horace E. Scudder. 7 vols. Boston: Houghton Mifflin, 1888–89, reissued 1904.

———. *The Complete Poetical Works of John Greenleaf Whittier* (Cambridge Edition). Boston: Houghton Mifflin, 1894.

———. *Whittier on Writers and Writing: The Uncollected Critical Writings of John Greenleaf Whittier*, ed. Edwin H. Cady and Harry Hayden Clark. Syracuse: Syracuse University Press, 1950.

———. *Legends of New England.* Gainesville, Fla.: Scholars' Facsimiles and Reprints, 1965.

Selected Poems

Massachusetts
to Virginia

Written on reading an account of the proceedings of the citizens of
Norfolk, Va., in reference to George Latimer, the alleged fugitive slave,
who was seized in Boston without warrant at the request of James B.
Grey, of Norfolk, claiming to be his master. The case caused great
excitement North and South, and led to the presentation of a petition
to Congress, signed by more than fifty thousand citizens of Massachusetts, calling for such laws and proposed amendments to the Constitution as should relieve the Commonwealth from all further participation
in the crime of oppression. George Latimer himself was finally given
free papers for the sum of four hundred dollars.

The blast from Freedom's Northern hills, upon its
     Southern way,
Bears greeting to Virginia from Massachusetts Bay:
No word of haughty challenging, nor battle-bugle's peal,
Nor steady tread of marching files, nor clang of
     horsemen's steel.

No trains of deep-mouthed cannon along our
     highways go;
Around our silent arsenals untrodden lies the snow;
And to the land-breeze of our ports, upon their
     errands far,
A thousand sails of commerce swell, but none are
     spread for war.

We hear thy threats, Virginia! thy stormy words
     and high,
Swell harshly on the Southern winds which melt
     along our sky;
Yet, not one brown, hard hand foregoes its honest
     labor here,
No hewer of our mountain oaks suspends his
     axe in fear.

Wild are the waves which lash the reefs along
    St. George's bank;
Cold on the shore of Labrador the fog lies white
    and dank;
Through storm, and wave, and blinding mist, stout are
    the hearts which man
The fishing-smacks of Marblehead, the sea-boats
    of Cape Ann.

The cold north light and wintry sun glare on their
    icy forms,
Bent grimly o'er their straining lines or wrestling with
    the storms;
Free as the winds they drive before, rough as the
    waves they roam,
They laugh to scorn the slaver's threat against
    their rocky home.

What means the Old Dominion? Hath she forgot
    the day
When o'er her conquered valleys swept the Briton's
    steel array?
How side by side, with sons of hers, the Massachusetts
    men
Encountered Tarleton's charge of fire, and stout
    Cornwallis, then?

Forgets she how the Bay State, in answer to the call
Of her old House of Burgesses, spoke out from
    Faneuil Hall?
When, echoing back her Henry's cry, came pulsing
    on each breath
Of Northern winds, the thrilling sounds of
    "Liberty or Death!"

What asks the Old Dominion? If now her sons
    have proved
False to their fathers' memory, false to the faith
    they loved;

If she can scoff at Freedom, and its great charter
    spurn,
Must we of Massachusetts from truth and
    duty turn?

We hunt your bondmen, flying from Slavery's
    hateful hell;
Our voices, at your bidding, take up the
    bloodhound's yell;
We gather, at your summons, above our fathers'
    graves,
From Freedom's holy altar-horns to tear your
    wretched slaves!

Thank God! not yet so vilely can Massachusetts bow;
The spirit of her early time is with her even now;
Dream not because her Pilgrim blood moves slow
    and calm and cool,
She thus can stoop her chainless neck, a sister's
    slave and tool!

All that a sister State should do, all that a free
    State may,
Heart, hand, and purse we proffer, as in our early day;
But that one dark loathsome burden ye must
    stagger with alone,
And reap the bitter harvest which ye yourselves
    have sown!

Hold, while ye may, your struggling slaves, and
    burden God's free air
With woman's shriek beneath the lash, and
    manhood's wild despair;
Cling closer to the "cleaving curse" that writes
    upon your plains
The blasting of Almighty wrath against a land
    of chains.

Still shame your gallant ancestry, the cavaliers
    of old,
By watching round the shambles where human
    flesh is sold;

Gloat o'er the new-born child, and count his
    market value, when
The maddened mother's cry of woe shall pierce the
    slaver's den!

Lower than plummet soundeth, sink the Virginia
    name;
Plant, if ye will, your fathers' graves with rankest
    weeds of shame;
Be, if ye will, the scandal of God's fair universe;
We wash our hands forever of your sin and shame
    and curse.

A voice from lips whereon the coal from Freedom's
    shrine hath been,
Thrilled, as but yesterday, the hearts of Berkshire's
    mountain men:
The echoes of that solemn voice are sadly lingering still
In all our sunny valleys, on every wind-swept hill.

And when the prowling man-thief came hunting
    for his prey
Beneath the very shadow of Bunker's shaft
    of gray,
How, through the free lips of the son, the father's
    warning spoke;
How, from its bonds of trade and sect, the Pilgrim
    city broke!

A hundred thousand right arms were lifted up
    on high,
A hundred thousand voices sent back their
    loud reply;
Through the thronged towns of Essex the startling
    summons rang,
And up from bench and loom and wheel her young
    mechanics sprang!

The voice of free, broad Middlesex, of thousands
    as of one,
The shaft of Bunker calling to that of Lexington;

From Norfolk's ancient villages, from Plymouth's
    rocky bound
To where Nantucket feels the arms of ocean close
    her round;

From rich and rural Worcester, where through the
    calm repose
Of cultured vales and fringing woods the gentle
    Nashua flows,
To where Wachuset's wintry blasts the mountain
    larches stir,
Swelled up to Heaven the thrilling cry of "God
    save Latimer!"

And sandy Barnstable rose up, wet with the salt
    sea spray;
And Bristol sent her answering shout down
    Narragansett Bay!
Along the broad Connecticut old Hampden felt
    the thrill,
And the cheer of Hampshire's woodmen swept
    down from Holyoke Hill.

The voice of Massachusetts! Of her free sons and
    daughters,
Deep calling unto deep aloud, the sound of many
    waters!
Against the burden of that voice what tyrant power
    shall stand?
No fetters in the Bay State! No slave upon
    her land!

Look to it well, Virginians! In calmness we
    have borne,
In answer to our faith and trust, your insult and
    your scorn;
You've spurned our kindest counsels; you've
    hunted for our lives;
And shaken round our hearths and homes your
    manacles and gyves!

We wage no war, we lift no arm, we fling no torch
within
The fire-damps of the quaking mine beneath your
soil of sin;
We leave ye with your bondmen, to wrestle, while
ye can,
With the strong upward tendencies and godlike
soul of man!

But for us and for our children, the vow which we
have given
For freedom and humanity is registered in heaven;
No slave-hunt in our borders, — no pirate on
our strand!
No fetters in the Bay State, — no slave upon
our land!

1843.

70

Song of Slaves
in the Desert

"*Sebah, Oasis of Fezzan*, 10*th March*, 1846. — This evening the female slaves were unusually excited in singing, and I had the curiosity to ask my negro servant, Said, what they were singing about. As many of them were natives of his own country, he had no difficulty in translating the Mandara or Bornou language. I had often asked the Moors to translate their songs for me, but got no satisfactory account from them. Said at first said, 'Oh, they sing of *Rubee*' (God). 'What do you mean?' I replied, impatiently. 'Oh, don't you know?' he continued, 'they asked God to give them their *Atka*?' (certificate of freedom). I inquired, 'Is that all?' Said: 'No; they say, "Where are we going? The world is large. *O God! Where are we going? O God!*"' I inquired, 'What else?' Said: 'They remember their country, Bornou, and say, "*Bornou was a pleasant country, full of all good things; but this is a bad country, and we are miserable!*"' 'Do they say anything else?' Said: 'No; they repeat these words over and over again, and add, "O God! give us our *Atka, and let us return again to our dear home.*"'

"I am not surprised I got little satisfaction when I asked the Moors about the songs of their slaves. Who will say that the above words are not a very appropriate song? What could have been more congenially adapted to their then woful condition? It is not to be wondered at that these poor bondwomen cheer up their hearts, in their long, lonely, and painful wanderings over the desert, with words and sentiments like these; but I have often observed that their fatigue and sufferings were too great for them to strike up this melancholy dirge, and many days their plaintive strains never broke over the silence of the desert." — *Richardson's Journal in Africa.*

Where are we going? where are we going,
    Where are we going, Rubee?

Lord of peoples, lord of lands,
Look across these shining sands,
Through the furnace of the noon,
Through the white light of the moon.
Strong the Ghiblee wind is blowing,
Strange and large the world is growing!
Speak and tell us where we are going,
    Where are we going, Rubee?

Bornou land was rich and good,
Wells of water, fields of food,
Dourra fields, and bloom of bean,
And the palm-tree cool and green:
Bornou land we see no longer,
Here we thirst and here we hunger,
Here the Moor-man smites in anger:
    Where are we going, Rubee?

When we went from Bornou land,
We were like the leaves and sand,
We were many, we are few;
Life has one, and death has two:
Whitened bones our path are showing,
Thou All-seeing, thou All-knowing!
Hear us, tell us, where are we going,
    Where are we going, Rubee?

Moons of marches from our eyes
Bornou land behind us lies;
Stranger round us day by day
Bends the desert circle gray;
Wild the waves of sand are flowing,
Hot the winds above them blowing, —
Lord of all things! where are we going?
    Where are we going, Rubee?

We are weak, but Thou art strong;
Short our lives, but Thine is long;
We are blind, but Thou hast eyes;
We are fools, but Thou art wise!
Thou, our morrow's pathway knowing
Through the strange world round us growing,
Hear us, tell us where are we going,
    Where are we going, Rubee?

1847.

Randolph of Roanoke

O Mother Earth! upon thy lap
   Thy weary ones receiving,
And o'er them, silent as a dream,
   Thy grassy mantle weaving,
Fold softly in thy long embrace
   That heart so worn and broken,
And cool its pulse of fire beneath
   Thy shadows old and oaken.

Shut out from him the bitter word
   And serpent hiss of scorning;
Nor let the storms of yesterday
   Disturb his quiet morning.
Breathe over him forgetfulness
   Of all save deeds of kindness,
And, save to smiles of grateful eyes,
   Press down his lids in blindness.

There, where with living ear and eye
   He heard Potomac's flowing,
And, through his tall ancestral trees,
   Saw autumn's sunset glowing,
He sleeps, still looking to the west,
   Beneath the dark wood shadow,
As if he still would see the sun
   Sink down on wave and meadow.

Bard, Sage, and Tribune! in himself
   All moods of mind contrasting, —
The tenderest wail of human woe,
   The scorn like lightning blasting;
The pathos which from rival eyes
   Unwilling tears could summon,
The stinging taunt, the fiery burst
   Of hatred scarcely human!

Mirth, sparkling like a diamond shower,
    From lips of life-long sadness;
Clear picturings of majestic thought
    Upon a ground of madness;
And over all Romance and Song
    A classic beauty throwing,
And laurelled Clio at his side
    Her storied pages showing.

All parties feared him: each in turn
    Beheld its schemes disjointed,
As right or left his fatal glance
    And spectral finger pointed.
Sworn foe of Cant, he smote it down
    With trenchant wit unsparing,
And, mocking, rent with ruthless hand
    The robe Pretence was wearing.

Too honest or too proud to feign
    A love he never cherished,
Beyond Virginia's border line
    His patriotism perished.
While others hailed in distant skies
    Our eagle's dusky pinion,
He only saw the mountain bird
    Stoop o'er his Old Dominion!

Still through each change of fortune strange,
    Racked nerve, and brain all burning,
His loving faith in Mother-land
    Knew never shade of turning;
By Britain's lakes, by Neva's tide,
    Whatever sky was o'er him,
He heard her rivers' rushing sound,
    Her blue peaks rose before him.

He held his slaves, yet made withal
    No false and vain pretences,
Nor paid a lying priest to seek
    For Scriptural defences.

His harshest words of proud rebuke,
  His bitterest taunt and scorning,
Fell fire-like on the Northern brow
  That bent to him in fawning.

He held his slaves; yet kept the while
  His reverence for the Human;
In the dark vassals of his will
  He saw but Man and Woman!
No hunter of God's outraged poor
  His Roanoke valley entered;
No trader in the souls of men
  Across his threshold ventured.

And when the old and wearied man
  Lay down for his last sleeping,
And at his side, a slave no more,
  His brother-man stood weeping,
His latest thought, his latest breath,
  To Freedom's duty giving,
With failing tongue and trembling hand
  The dying blest the living.

Oh, never bore his ancient State
  A truer son or braver!
None trampling with a calmer scorn
  On foreign hate or favor.
He knew her faults, yet never stooped
  His proud and manly feeling
To poor excuses of the wrong
  Or meanness of concealing.

But none beheld with clearer eye
  The plague-spot o'er her spreading,
None heard more sure the steps of Doom
  Along her future treading.
For her as for himself he spake,
  When, his gaunt frame upbracing,
He traced with dying hand "Remorse!"
  And perished in the tracing.

As from the grave where Henry sleeps,
From Vernon's weeping willow,
And from the grassy pall which hides
The Sage of Monticello,
So from the leaf-strewn burial-stone
Of Randolph's lowly dwelling,
Virginia! o'er thy land of slaves
A warning voice is swelling!

And hark! from thy deserted fields
Are sadder warnings spoken,
From quenched hearths, where thy exiled sons
Their household gods have broken.
The curse is on thee, — wolves for men,
And briers for corn-sheaves giving!
Oh, more than all thy dead renown
Were now one hero living!

1847.

To My Sister

With a Copy of "The Supernaturalism
of New England."

The work referred to was a series of papers under this title, contributed
to the *Democratic Review* and afterward collected into a volume, in
which I noted some of the superstitions and folklore prevalent in New
England. The volume has not been kept in print, but most of its con-
tents are distributed in my *Literary Recreations and Miscellanies.*

Dear Sister! while the wise and sage
Turn coldly from my playful page,
And count it strange that ripened age
   Should stoop to boyhood's folly;
I know that thou wilt judge aright
Of all which makes the heart more light,
Or lends one star-gleam to the night
   Of clouded Melancholy.

Away with weary cares and themes!
Swing wide the moonlit gate of dreams!
Leave free once more the land which teems
   With wonders and romances!
Where thou, with clear discerning eyes,
Shalt rightly read the truth which lies
Beneath the quaintly masking guise
   Of wild and wizard fancies.

Lo! once again our feet we set
On still green wood-paths, twilight wet,
By lonely brooks, whose waters fret
   The roots of spectral beeches;
Again the hearth-fire glimmers o'er
Home's whitewashed wall and painted floor,
And young eyes widening to the lore
   Of faery-folks and witches.

Dear heart! the legend is not vain
Which lights that holy hearth again,
And calling back from care and pain,
   And death's funereal sadness,
Draws round its old familiar blaze
The clustering groups of happier days,
And lends to sober manhood's gaze
   A glimpse of childish gladness.

And, knowing how my life hath been
A weary work of tongue and pen,
A long, harsh strife with strong-willed men,
   Thou wilt not chide my turning
To con, at times, an idle rhyme,
To pluck a flower from childhood's clime,
Or listen, at Life's noonday chime,
   For the sweet bells of Morning!

1847.

Ichabod

This poem was the outcome of the surprise and grief and forecast of evil consequences which I felt on reading the seventh of March speech of Daniel Webster in support of the "compromise," and the Fugitive Slave Law. No partisan or personal enmity dictated it. On the contrary my admiration of the splendid personality and intellectual power f the great Senator was never stronger than when I laid down his speech, and, in one of the saddest moments of my life penned my protest. I saw, as I wrote, with painful clearness its sure results, — the Slave Power arrogant and defiant, strengthened and encouraged to carry out its scheme for the extension of its baleful system, or the dissolution of the Union, the guaranties of personal liberty in the free States broken down, and the whole country made the hunting-ground of slave-catchers. In the horror of such a vision, so soon fearfully fulfilled, if one spoke at all, he could only speak in tones of stern and sorrowful rebuke.

But death softens all resentments, and the consciousness of a common inheritance of frailty and weakness modifies the severity of judgment. Years after, in *The Lost Occasion* I gave utterance to an almost universal regret that the great statesman did not live to see the flag which he loved trampled under the feet of Slavery, and, in view of this desecration, make his last days glorious in defence of "Liberty and Union, one and inseparable."

So fallen! so lost! the light withdrawn
    Which once he wore!
The glory from his gray hairs gone
    Forevermore!

Revile him not, the Tempter hath
    A snare for all;
And pitying tears, not scorn and wrath,
    Befit his fall!

Oh, dumb be passion's stormy rage,
    When he who might
Have lighted up and led his age,
    Falls back in night.

Scorn! would the angels laugh, to mark
    A bright soul driven,
Fiend-goaded, down the endless dark,
    From hope and heaven!

Let not the land once proud of him
    Insult him now,
Nor brand with deeper shame his dim,
    Dishonored brow.

But let its humbled sons, instead,
    From sea to lake,
A long lament, as for the dead,
    In sadness make.

Of all we loved and honored, naught
    Save power remains;
A fallen angel's pride of thought,
    Still strong in chains.

All else is gone; from those great eyes
    The soul has fled:
When faith is lost, when honor dies,
    The man is dead!

Then, pay the reverence of old days
    To his dead fame;
Walk backward, with averted gaze,
    And hide the shame!

1850.

To My Old Schoolmaster

An Epistle Not After the Manner of Horace.

These lines were addressed to my worthy friend Joshua Coffin, teacher, historian, and antiquarian. He was one of the twelve persons who with William Lloyd Garrison formed the first anti-slavery society in New England.

Old friend, kind friend! lightly down
Drop time's snow-flakes on thy crown!
Never be thy shadow less,
Never fail thy cheerfulness;
Care, that kills the cat, may plough
Wrinkles in the miser's brow,
Deepen envy's spiteful frown,
Draw the mouths of bigots down,
Plague ambition's dream, and sit
Heavy on the hypocrite,
Haunt the rich man's door, and ride
In the gilded coach of pride; —
Let the fiend pass! — what can he
Find to do with such as thee?
Seldom comes that evil guest
Where the conscience lies at rest,
And brown health and quiet wit
Smiling on the threshold sit.

I, the urchin unto whom,
In that smoked and dingy room,
Where the district gave thee rule
O'er its ragged winter school,
Thou didst teach the mysteries
Of those weary A B C's, —
Where, to fill the every pause
Of thy wise and learned saws,
Through the cracked and crazy wall

Came the cradle-rock and squall,
And the goodman's voice, at strife
With his shrill and tipsy wife, —
Luring us by stories old,
With a comic unction told,
More than by the eloquence
Of terse birchen arguments
(Doubtful gain, I fear), to look
With complacence on a book! —
Where the genial pedagogue
Half forgot his rogues to flog,
Citing tale or apologue,
Wise and merry in its drift
As was Phædrus' twofold gift,
Had the little rebels known it,
Risum et prudentiam monet!
I, — the man of middle years,
In whose sable locks appears
Many a warning fleck of gray, —
Looking back to that far day,
And thy primal lessons, feel
Grateful smiles my lips unseal,
As, remembering thee, I blend
Olden teacher, present friend,
Wise with antiquarian search,
In the scrolls of State and Church:
Named on history's title-page,
Parish-clerk and justice sage;
For the ferule's wholesome awe
Wielding now the sword of law.

Threshing Time's neglected sheaves,
Gathering up the scattered leaves
Which the wrinkled sibyl cast
Careless from her as she passed, —
Twofold citizen art thou,
Freeman of the past and now.
He who bore thy name of old
Midway in the heavens did hold
Over Gibeon moon and sun;
Thou hast bidden them backward run;

Of to-day the present ray
Flinging over yesterday!

Let the busy ones deride
What I deem of right thy pride:
Let the fools their treadmills grind,
Look not forward nor behind,
Shuffle in and wriggle out,
Veer with every breeze about,
Turning like a windmill sail,
Or a dog that seeks his tail;
Let them laugh to see thee fast
Tabernacled in the Past,
Working out with eye and lip,
Riddles of old penmanship,
Patient as Belzoni there
Sorting out, with loving care,
Mummies of dead questions stripped
From their sevenfold manuscript!

Dabbling, in their noisy way,
In the puddles of to-day,
Little know they of that vast
Solemn ocean of the past,
On whose margin, wreck-bespread,
Thou art walking with the dead,
Questioning the stranded years,
Waking smiles, by turns, and tears,
As thou callest up again
Shapes the dust has long o'erlain, —
Fair-haired woman, bearded man,
Cavalier and Puritan;
In an age whose eager view
Seeks but present things, and new,
Mad for party, sect and gold,
Teaching reverence for the old.

On that shore, with fowler's tact,
Coolly bagging fact on fact,
Naught amiss to thee can float,
Tale, or song, or anecdote;

Village gossip, centuries old,
Scandals by our grandams told,
What the pilgrim's table spread,
Where he lived, and whom he wed,
Long-drawn bill of wine and beer
For his ordination cheer,
Or the flip that wellnigh made
Glad his funeral cavalcade;
Weary prose, and poet's lines,
Flavored by their age, like wines,
Eulogistic of some quaint,
Doubtful, puritanic saint;
Lays that quickened husking jigs,
Jests that shook grave periwigs,
When the parson had his jokes
And his glass, like other folks;
Sermons that, for mortal hours,
Taxed our fathers' vital powers,
As the long nineteenthlies poured
Downward from the sounding-board,
And, for fire of Pentecost,
Touched their beards December's frost.

Time is hastening on, and we
What our fathers are shall be, —
Shadow-shapes of memory!
Joined to that vast multitude
Where the great are but the good,
And the mind of strength shall prove
Weaker than the heart of love;
Pride of graybeard wisdom less
Than the infant's guilelessness,
And his song of sorrow more
Than the crown the Psalmist wore!
Who shall then, with pious zeal,
At our moss-grown thresholds kneel,
From a stained and stony page
Reading to a careless age,
With a patient eye like thine,
Prosing tale and limping line,

Names and words the hoary rime
Of the Past has made sublime?
Who shall work for us as well
The antiquarian's miracle?
Who to seeming life recall
Teacher grave and pupil small?
Who shall give to thee and me
Freeholds in futurity?

Well, whatever lot be mine,
Long and happy days be thine,
Ere thy full and honored age
Dates of time its latest page!
Squire for master, State for school,
Wisely lenient, live and rule;
Over grown-up knave and rogue
Play the watchful pedagogue;
Or, while pleasure smiles on duty,
At the call of youth and beauty,
Speak for them the spell of law
Which shall bar and bolt withdraw,
And the flaming sword remove
From the Paradise of Love.
Still, with undimmed eyesight, pore
Ancient tome and record o'er;
Still thy week-day lyrics croon,
Pitch in church the Sunday tune,
Showing something, in thy part,
Of the old Puritanic art,
Singer after Sternhold's heart!
In thy pew, for many a year,
Homilies from Oldbug hear,
Who to wit like that of South,
And the Syrian's golden mouth,
Doth the homely pathos add
Which the pilgrim preachers had;
Breaking, like a child at play,
Gilded idols of the day,
Cant of knave and pomp of fool
Tossing with his ridicule,

Yet, in earnest or in jest,
Ever keeping truth abreast.
And, when thou art called, at last,
To thy townsmen of the past,
Not as stranger shalt thou come;
Thou shalt find thyself at home
With the little and the big,
Woollen cap and periwig,
Madam in her high-laced ruff,
Goody in her home-made stuff, —
Wise and simple, rich and poor,
Thou hast known them all before!

1851.

First-Day Thoughts

In calm and cool and silence, once again
  I find my old accustomed place among
  My brethren, where, perchance, no human tongue
  Shall utter words; where never hymn is sung,
  Nor deep-toned organ blown, nor censer swung,
Nor dim light falling through the pictured pane!
There, syllabled by silence, let me hear
The still small voice which reached the prophet's ear;
Read in my heart a still diviner law
Than Israel's leader on his tables saw!
There let me strive with each besetting sin,
  Recall my wandering fancies, and restrain
  The sore disquiet of a restless brain;
  And, as the path of duty is made plain,
May grace be given that I may walk therein,
  Not like the hireling, for his selfish gain,
With backward glances and reluctant tread,
Making a merit of his coward dread,
  But, cheerful, in the light around me thrown,
  Walking as one to pleasant service led;
  Doing God's will as if it were my own,
Yet trusting not in mine, but in His strength
    alone!

1852.

Trust

The same old baffling questions! O my friend,
I cannot answer them. In vain I send
My soul into the dark, where never burn
   The lamps of science, nor the natural light
Of Reason's sun and stars! I cannot learn
Their great and solemn meanings, nor discern
The awful secrets of the eyes which turn
   Evermore on us through the day and night
   With silent challenge and a dumb demand,
Proffering the riddles of the dread unknown,
Like the calm Sphinxes, with their eyes of stone,
   Questioning the centuries from their veils
     of sand!
I have no answer for myself or thee,
Save that I learned beside my mother's knee;
"All is of God that is, and is to be;
   And God is good." Let this suffice us still,
   Resting in childlike trust upon His will
Who moves to His great ends unthwarted
     by the ill.

1853.

Maud Muller

The recollection of some descendants of a Hessian deserter in the Revolutionary war bearing the name of Muller doubtless suggested the somewhat infelicitous title of a New England idyl. The poem had no real foundation in fact, though a hint of it may have been found in recalling an incident, trivial in itself, of a journey on the picturesque Maine seaboard with my sister some years before it was written. We had stopped to rest our tired horse under the shade of an apple tree, and refresh him with water from a little brook which rippled through the stone wall across the road. A very beautiful young girl in scantest summer attire was at work in the hay-field, and as we talked with her we noticed that she strove to hide her bare feet by raking hay over them, blushing as she did so, through the tan of her cheek and neck.

Maud Muller on a summer's day,
Raked the meadow sweet with hay.

Beneath her torn hat glowed the wealth
Of simple beauty and rustic health.

Singing, she wrought, and her merry glee
The mock-bird echoed from his tree.

But when she glanced to the far-off town,
White from its hill-slope looking down,

The sweet song died, and a vague unrest
And a nameless longing filled her breast, —

A wish, that she hardly dared to own,
For something better than she had known.

The Judge rode slowly down the lane,
Smoothing his horse's chestnut mane.

He drew his bridle in the shade
Of the apple-trees, to greet the maid,

And asked a draught from the spring that flowed
Through the meadow across the road.

She stooped where the cool spring bubbled up,
And filled for him her small tin cup,

And blushed as she gave it, looking down
On her feet so bare, and her tattered gown.

"Thanks!" said the Judge; "a sweeter draught
From a fairer hand was never quaffed."

He spoke of the grass and flowers and trees,
Of the singing birds and the humming bees;

Then talked of the haying, and wondered whether
The cloud in the west would bring foul weather.

And Maud forgot her brier-torn gown,
And her graceful ankles bare and brown;

And listened, while a pleased surprise
Looked from her long-lashed hazel eyes.

At last, like one who for delay
Seeks a vain excuse, he rode away.

Maud Muller looked and sighed: "Ah me!
That I the Judge's bride might be!

"He would dress me up in silks so fine,
And praise and toast me at his wine.

"My father should wear a broadcloth coat;
My brother should sail a painted boat.

"I'd dress my mother so grand and gay,
And the baby should have a new toy each day.

"And I'd feed the hungry and clothe the poor,
And all should bless me who left our door."

The Judge looked back as he climbed the hill,
And saw Maud Muller standing still.

"A form more fair, a face more sweet,
Ne'er hath it been my lot to meet.

"And her modest answer and graceful air
Show her wise and good as she is fair.

"Would she were mine, and I to-day,
Like her, a harvester of hay;

"No doubtful balance of rights and wrongs,
Nor weary lawyers with endless tongues,

"But low of cattle and song of birds,
And health and quiet and loving words."

But he thought of his sisters, proud and cold,
And his mother, vain of her rank and gold.

So, closing his heart, the Judge rode on,
And Maud was left in the field alone.

But the lawyers smiled that afternoon,
When he hummed in court an old love-tune;

And the young girl mused beside the well
Till the rain on the unraked clover fell.

He wedded a wife of richest dower,
Who lived for fashion, as he for power.

Yet oft, in his marble hearth's bright glow,
He watched a picture come and go;

And sweet Maud Muller's hazel eyes
Looked out in their innocent surprise.

Oft, when the wine in his glass was red,
He longed for the wayside well instead;

And closed his eyes on his garnished rooms
To dream of meadows and clover-blooms.

And the proud man sighed, with a secret pain,
"Ah, that I were free again!

"Free as when I rode that day,
Where the barefoot maiden raked her hay."

She wedded a man unlearned and poor,
And many children played round her door.

But care and sorrow, and childbirth pain,
Left their traces on heart and brain.

And oft, when the summer sun shone hot
On the new-mown hay in the meadow lot,

And she heard the little spring brook fall
Over the roadside, through the wall,

In the shade of the apple-tree again
She saw a rider draw his rein.

And, gazing down with timid grace,
She felt his pleased eyes read her face.

Sometimes her narrow kitchen walls
Stretched away into stately halls;

The weary wheel to a spinnet turned,
The tallow candle an astral burned,

And for him who sat by the chimney lug,
Dozing and grumbling o'er pipe and mug,

A manly form at her side she saw,
And joy was duty and love was law.

Then she took up her burden of life again,
Saying only, "It might have been."

Alas for maiden, alas for Judge,
For rich repiner and household drudge!

God pity them both! and pity us all,
Who vainly the dreams of youth recall.

For all of sad words of tongue or pen,
The saddest are these: "It might have been!"

Ah, well! for us all some sweet hope lies
Deeply buried from human eyes;

And, in the hereafter, angels may
Roll the stone from its grave away!

1854.

Letter

*From A Missionary of the Methodist
Episcopal Church South,
In Kansas, To A Distinguished Politician.*
Douglas Mission, *August*, 1854.

Last week — the Lord be praised for all
    His mercies
To His unworthy servant! — I arrived
Safe at the Mission, *via* Westport; where
I tarried over night, to aid in forming
A Vigilance Committee, to send back,
In shirts of tar, and feather-doublets quilted
With forty stripes save one, all Yankee comers,
Uncircumcised and Gentile, aliens from
The Commonwealth of Israel, who despise
The prize of the high calling of the saints,
Who plant amidst this heathen wilderness
Pure gospel institutions, sanctified
By patriarchal use. The meeting opened
With prayer, as was most fitting. Half an hour,
Or thereaway, I groaned, and strove, and wrestled,
As Jacob did at Penuel, till the power
Fell on the people, and they cried "Amen!"
"Glory to God!" and stamped and clapped
    their hands;
And the rough river boatmen wiped their eyes;
"Go it, old hoss!" they cried, and cursed the
    niggers —
Fulfilling thus the word of prophecy,
"Cursed be Canaan." After prayer, the meeting
Chose a committee — good and pious men —
A Presbyterian Elder, Baptist deacon,
A local preacher, three or four class-leaders,
Anxious inquirers, and renewed backsliders,

A score in all — to watch the river ferry,
(As they of old did watch the fords of Jordan,)
And cut off all whose Yankee tongues refuse
The Shibboleth of the Nebraska bill.
And then, in answer to repeated calls,
I gave a brief account of what I saw
In Washington; and truly many hearts
Rejoiced to know the President, and you
And all the Cabinet regularly hear
The gospel message of a Sunday morning,
Drinking with thirsty souls of the sincere
Milk of the Word. Glory! Amen, and Selah!

Here, at the Mission, all things have gone well:
The brother who, throughout my absence, acted
As overseer, assures me that the crops
Never were better. I have lost one negro,
A first-rate hand, but obstinate and sullen.
He ran away some time last spring, and hid
In the river timber. There my Indian converts
Found him, and treed and shot him. For the rest,
The heathens round about begin to feel
The influence of our pious ministrations
And works of love; and some of them already
Have purchased negroes, and are settling down
As sober Christians! Bless the Lord for this!
I know it will rejoice you. You, I hear,
Are on the eve of visiting Chicago,
To fight with the wild beasts of Ephesus,
Long John, and Dutch Free-Soilers.
      May your arm
Be clothed with strength, and on your tongue be
      found
The sweet oil of persuasion. So desires
Your brother and co-laborer. Amen!

  P.S. All's lost. Even while I write
      these lines,
The Yankee abolitionists are coming
Upon us like a flood — grim, stalwart men,
Each face set like a flint of Plymouth Rock
Against our institutions — staking out

Their farm lots on the wooded Wakarusa,
Or squatting by the mellow-bottomed Kansas;
The pioneers of mightier multitudes,
The small rain-patter, ere the thunder shower
Drowns the dry prairies. Hope from man is not.
Oh, for a quiet berth at Washington,
Snug naval chaplaincy, or clerkship, where
These rumors of free labor and free soil
Might never meet me more. Better to be
Door-keeper in the White House, than to dwell
Amidst these Yankee tents, that, whitening, show
On the green prairie like a fleet becalmed.
Methinks I hear a voice come up the river
From those far bayous, where the alligators
Mount guard around the camping filibusters:
"Shake off the dust of Kansas. Turn to Cuba —
(That golden orange just about to fall,
O'er-ripe, into the Democratic lap;)
Keep pace with Providence, or, as we say,
Manifest destiny. Go forth and follow
The message of *our* gospel, thither borne
Upon the point of Quitman's bowie-knife,
And the persuasive lips of Colt's revolvers.
There may'st thou, underneath thy vine and
        fig-tree,
Watch thy increase of sugar cane and negroes,
Calm as a patriarch in his eastern tent!"
Amen: So mote it be. So prays your friend.

1854.

96

The Barefoot Boy

Blessings on thee, little man,
Barefoot boy, with cheek of tan!
With thy turned-up pantaloons,
And thy merry whistled tunes;
With thy red lip, redder still
Kissed by strawberries on the hill;
With the sunshine on thy face,
Through thy torn brim's jaunty grace;
From my heart I give thee joy, —
I was once a barefoot boy!
Prince thou art, — the grown-up man
Only is republican.
Let the million-dollared ride!
Barefoot, trudging at his side,
Thou hast more than he can buy
In the reach of ear and eye, —
Outward sunshine, inward joy:
Blessings on thee, barefoot boy!

Oh for boyhood's painless play,
Sleep that wakes in laughing day,
Health that mocks the doctor's rules,
Knowledge never learned of schools,
Of the wild bee's morning chase,
Of the wild-flower's time and place,
Flight of fowl and habitude
Of the tenants of the wood;
How the tortoise bears his shell,
How the woodchuck digs his cell,
And the ground-mole sinks his well;
How the robin feeds her young,
How the oriole's nest is hung;
Where the whitest lilies blow,

Where the freshest berries grow,
Where the ground-nut trails its vine,
Where the wood-grape's clusters shine;
Of the black wasp's cunning way,
Mason of his walls of clay,
And the architectural plans
Of gray hornet artisans!
For, eschewing books and tasks,
Nature answers all he asks;
Hand in hand with her he walks,
Face to face with her he talks,
Part and parcel of her joy, —
Blessings on the barefoot boy!

Oh for boyhood's time of June,
Crowding years in one brief moon,
When all things I heard or saw,
Me, their master, waited for.
I was rich in flowers and trees,
Humming-birds and honey-bees;
For my sport the squirrel played,
Plied the snouted mole his spade;
For my taste the blackberry cone
Purpled over hedge and stone;
Laughed the brook for my delight
Through the day and through the night,
Whispering at the garden wall,
Talked with me from fall to fall;
Mine the sand-rimmed pickerel pond,
Mine the walnut slopes beyond,
Mine, on bending orchard trees,
Apples of Hesperides!
Still as my horizon grew,
Larger grew my riches too;
All the world I saw or knew
Seemed a complex Chinese toy,
Fashioned for a barefoot boy!

Oh for festal dainties spread,
Like my bowl of milk and bread;
Pewter spoon and bowl of wood,
On the door-stone, gray and rude!

O'er me, like a regal tent,
Cloudy-ribbed, the sunset bent,
Purple-curtained, fringed with gold,
Looped in many a wind-swung fold;
While for music came the play
Of the pied frogs' orchestra;
And, to light the noisy choir,
Lit the fly his lamp of fire.
I was monarch: pomp and joy
Waited on the barefoot boy!

Cheerily, then, my little man,
Live and laugh, as boyhood can!
Though the flinty slopes be hard,
Stubble-speared the new-mown sward,
Every morn shall lead thee through
Fresh baptisms of the dew;
Every evening from thy feet
Shall the cool wind kiss the heat:
All too soon these feet must hide
In the prison cells of pride,
Lose the freedom of the sod,
Like a colt's for work be shod,
Made to tread the mills of toil,
Up and down in ceaseless moil:
Happy if their track be found
Never on forbidden ground;
Happy if they sink not in
Quick and treacherous sands of sin.
Ah! that thou couldst know thy joy,
Ere it passes, barefoot boy!

1855.

The Panorama

"A! fredome is a nobill thing!
　Fredome mayse man to haif liking.
　Fredome all solace to man giffis;
　He levys at ese that frely levys!
　A nobil hart may haif mane ese
　Na ellys nocht that may him plese
　Gyff Fredome failythe."

ARCHDEACON BARBOUR

Through the long hall the shuttered windows shed
A dubious light on every upturned head;
On locks like those of Absalom the fair,
On the bald apex ringed with scanty hair,
On blank indifference and on curious stare;
On the pale Showman reading from his stage
The hieroglyphics of that facial page;
Half sad, half scornful, listening to the bruit
Of restless cane-tap and impatient foot,
And the shrill call, across the general din,
"Roll up your curtain! Let the show begin!"

At length a murmur like the winds that break
Into green waves the prairie's grassy lake,
Deepened and swelled to music clear and loud,
And, as the west-wind lifts a summer cloud,
The curtain rose, disclosing wide and far
A green land stretching to the evening star,
Fair rivers, skirted by primeval trees
And flowers hummed over by the desert bees,
Marked by tall bluffs whose slopes of
　　greenness show
Fantastic outcrops of the rock below;
The slow result of patient Nature's pains,
And plastic fingering of her sun and rains;

100

Arch, tower, and gate, grotesquely windowed
    hall,
And long escarpment of half-crumbled wall,
Huger than those which, from steep hills of vine,
Stare through their loopholes on the travelled
    Rhine;
Suggesting vaguely to the gazer's mind
A fancy, idle as the prairie wind,
Of the land's dwellers in an age unguessed;
The unsung Jotuns of the mystic West.

Beyond, the prairie's sea-like swells surpass
The Tartar's marvels of his Land of Grass,
Vast as the sky against whose sunset shores
Wave after wave the billowy greenness pours;
And, onward still, like islands in that main
Loom the rough peaks of many a mountain chain,
Whence east and west a thousand waters run
From winter lingering under summer's sun.
And, still beyond, long lines of foam and sand
Tell where Pacific rolls his waves a-land,
From many a wide-lapped port and land-locked bay,
Opening with thunderous pomp the world's highway
To Indian isles of spice, and marts of far Cathay.

"Such," said the Showman, as the curtain fell,
"Is the new Canaan of our Israel;
The land of promise to the swarming North,
Which, hive-like, sends its annual surplus forth,
To the poor Southron on his worn-out soil,
Scathed by the curses of unnatural toil;
To Europe's exiles seeking home and rest,
And the lank nomads of the wandering West,
Who, asking neither, in their love of change
And the free bison's amplitude of range,
Rear the log-hut, for present shelter meant,
Not future comfort, like an Arab's tent."

Then spake a shrewd on-looker, "Sir," said he,
"I like your picture, but I fain would see
A sketch of what your promised land will be
When, with electric nerve, and fiery-brained,

With Nature's forces to its chariot chained,
The future grasping, by the past obeyed,
The twentieth century rounds a new decade."

Then said the Showman, sadly: "He who grieves
Over the scattering of the sibyl's leaves
Unwisely mourns. Suffice it, that we know
What needs must ripen from the seed we sow;
That present time is but the mould wherein
We cast the shapes of holiness and sin.
A painful watcher of the passing hour,
Its lust of gold, its strife for place and power;
Its lack of manhood, honor, reverence, truth,
Wise-thoughted age, and generous-hearted youth;
Nor yet unmindful of each better sign,
The low, far lights, which on th' horizon shine,
Like those which sometimes tremble on the rim
Of clouded skies when day is closing dim,
Flashing athwart the purple spears of rain
The hope of sunshine on the hills again:
I need no prophet's word, nor shapes that pass
Like clouding shadows o'er a magic glass;
For now, as ever, passionless and cold,
Doth the dread angel of the future hold
Evil and good before us, with no voice
Or warning look to guide us in our choice;
With spectral hands outreaching through the gloom
The shadowy contrasts of the coming doom.
Transferred from these, it now remains to give
The sun and shade of Fate's alternative."

Then, with a burst of music, touching all
The keys of thrifty life, — the mill-stream's fall,
The engine's pant along its quivering rails,
The anvil's ring, the measured beat of flails,
The sweep of scythes, the reaper's whistled tune,
Answering the summons of the bells of noon,
The woodman's hail along the river shores,
The steamboat's signal, and the dip of oars:
Slowly the curtain rose from off a land
Fair as God's garden. Broad on either hand
The golden wheat-fields glimmered in the sun,

And the tall maize its yellow tassels spun.
Smooth highways set with hedge-rows living green,
With steepled towns through shaded vistas seen,
The school-house murmuring with its hive-like
    swarm,
The brook-bank whitening in the grist-mill's storm,
The painted farm-house shining through the leaves
Of fruited orchards bending at its eaves,
Where live again, around the Western hearth,
The homely old-time virtues of the North;
Where the blithe housewife rises with the day,
And well-paid labor counts his task a play.
And, grateful tokens of a Bible free,
And the free Gospel of Humanity,
Of diverse sects and differing names the shrines,
One in their faith, whate'er their outward signs,
Like varying strophes of the same sweet hymn
From many a prairie's swell and river's brim,
A thousand church-spires sanctify the air
Of the calm Sabbath, with their sign of prayer.

    Like sudden nightfall over bloom and green
The curtain dropped: and, momently, between
The clank of fetter and the crack of thong,
Half sob, half laughter, music swept along;
A strange refrain, whose idle words and low,
Like drunken mourners, kept the time of woe;
As if the revellers at a masquerade
Heard in the distance funeral marches played.
Such music, dashing all his smiles with tears,
The thoughtful voyager on Ponchartrain hears,
Where, through the noonday dusk of wooded shores
The negro boatman, singing to his oars,
With a wild pathos borrowed of his wrong
Redeems the jargon of his senseless song.
"Look," said the Showman, sternly, as he rolled
His curtain upward. "Fate's reverse behold!"

    A village straggling in loose disarray
Of vulgar newness, premature decay;
A tavern, crazy with its whiskey brawls,
With "*Slaves at Auction!*" garnishing its walls;

Without, surrounded by a motley crowd,
The shrewd-eyed salesman, garrulous and loud,
A squire or colonel in his pride of place,
Known at free fights, the caucus, and the race,
Prompt to proclaim his honor without blot,
And silence doubters with a ten-pace shot,
Mingling the negro-driving bully's rant
With pious phrase and democratic cant,
Yet never scrupling, with a filthy jest,
To sell the infant from its mother's breast,
Break through all ties of wedlock, home, and kin,
Yield shrinking girlhood up to graybeard sin;
Sell all the virtues with his human stock,
The Christian graces on his auction-block,
And coolly count on shrewdest bargains driven
In hearts regenerate, and in souls forgiven!

Look once again! The moving canvas shows
A slave plantation's slovenly repose,
Where, in rude cabins rotting midst their weeds,
The human chattel eats, and sleeps, and breeds;
And, held a brute, in practice, as in law,
Becomes in fact the thing he's taken for.
There, early summoned to the hemp and corn,
The nursing mother leaves her child new-born;
There haggard sickness, weak and deathly faint,
Crawls to his task, and fears to make complaint;
And sad-eyed Rachels, childless in decay,
Weep for their lost ones sold and torn away!
Of ampler size the master's dwelling stands,
In shabby keeping with his half-tilled lands;
The gates unhinged, the yard with weeds unclean,
The cracked veranda with a tipsy lean.
Without, loose-scattered like a wreck adrift,
Signs of misrule and tokens of unthrift;
Within, profusion to discomfort joined,
The listless body and the vacant mind;
The fear, the hate, the theft and falsehood, born
In menial hearts of toil, and stripes, and scorn!
There, all the vices, which, like birds obscene,
Batten on slavery loathsome and unclean,
From the foul kitchen to the parlor rise,

104

Pollute the nursery where the child-heir lies,
Taint infant lips beyond all after cure,
With the fell poison of a breast impure;
Touch boyhood's passions with the breath of flame,
From girlhood's instincts steal the blush of shame.
So swells, from low to high, from weak to strong,
The tragic chorus of the baleful wrong;
Guilty or guiltless, all within its range
Feel the blind justice of its sure revenge.

Still scenes like these the moving chart reveals.
Up the long western steppes the blighting steals;
Down the Pacific slope the evil Fate
Glides like a shadow to the Golden Gate:
From sea to sea the drear eclipse is thrown,
From sea to sea the *Mauvaises Terres* have grown,
A belt of curses on the New World's zone!

The curtain fell. All drew a freer breath,
As men are wont to do when mournful death
Is covered from their sight. The Showman stood
With drooping brow in sorrow's attitude
One moment, then with sudden gesture shook
His loose hair back, and with the air and look
Of one who felt, beyond the narrow stage
And listening group, the presence of the age,
And heard the footsteps of the things to be,
Poured out his soul in earnest words and free.

"O friends!" he said, "in this poor trick
    of paint
You see the semblance, incomplete and faint,
Of the two-fronted Future, which, to-day,
Stands dim and silent, waiting in your way.
To-day, your servant, subject to your will;
To-morrow, master, or for good or ill.
If the dark face of Slavery on you turns,
If the mad curse its paper barrier spurns,
If the world granary of the West is made
The last foul market of the slaver's trade,
Why rail at fate? The mischief is your own.
Why hate your neighbor? Blame yourselves alone!

105

"Men of the North! The South you charge
    with wrong
Is weak and poor, while you are rich and strong.
If questions, — idle and absurd as those
The old-time monks and Paduan doctors chose, —
Mere ghosts of questions, tariffs, and dead banks,
And scarecrow pontiffs, never broke your ranks,
Your thews united could, at once, roll back
The jostled nation to its primal track.
Nay, were you simply steadfast, manly, just,
True to the faith your fathers left in trust,
If stainless honor outweighed in your scale
A codfish quintal or a factory bale,
Full many a noble heart, (and such remain
In all the South, like Lot in Siddim's plain,
Who watch and wait, and from the wrong's control
Keep white and pure their chastity of soul,)
Now sick to loathing of your weak complaints,
Your tricks as sinners, and your prayers as saints,
Would half-way meet the frankness of your tone,
And feel their pulses beating with your own.

"The North! the South! no geographic line
Can fix the boundary or the point define,
Since each with each so closely interblends,
Where Slavery rises, and where Freedom ends.
Beneath your rocks the roots, far-reaching, hide
Of the fell Upas on the Southern side;
The tree whose branches in your northwinds wave
Dropped its young blossoms on Mount Vernon's
    grave;
The nursling growth of Monticello's crest
Is now the glory of the free Northwest;
To the wise maxims of her olden school
Virginia listened from thy lips, Rantoul;
Seward's words of power, and Sumner's fresh
    renown,
Flow from the pen that Jefferson laid down!
And when, at length, her years of madness o'er,
Like the crowned grazer on Euphrates' shore,
From her long lapse to savagery, her mouth
Bitter with baneful herbage, turns the South,

Resumes her old attire, and seeks to smooth
Her unkempt tresses at the glass of truth,
Her early faith shall find a tongue again,
New Wythes and Pinckneys swell that old refrain,
Her sons with yours renew the ancient pact,
The myth of Union prove at last a fact!
Then, if one murmur mars the wide content,
Some Northern lip will drawl the last dissent,
Some Union-saving patriot of your own
Lament to find his occupation gone.

"Grant that the North's insulted, scorned,
        betrayed,
O'erreached in bargains with her neighbor made,
When selfish thrift and party held the scales
For peddling dicker, not for honest sales, —
Whom shall we strike? Who most deserves
        our blame?
The braggart Southron, open in his aim,
And bold as wicked, crashing straight through all
That bars his purpose, like a cannon-ball?
Or the mean traitor, breathing northern air,
With nasal speech and puritanic hair,
Whose cant the loss of principle survives,
As the mud-turtle e'en its head outlives;
Who, caught, chin-buried in some foul offence,
Puts on a look of injured innocence,
And consecrates his baseness to the cause
Of constitution, union, and the laws?

"Praise to the place-man who can hold aloof
His still unpurchased manhood, office-proof;
Who on his round of duty walks erect,
And leaves it only rich in self-respect;
As More maintained his virtue's lofty port
In the Eighth Henry's base and bloody court.
But, if exceptions here and there are found,
Who tread thus safely on enchanted ground,
The normal type, the fitting symbol still
Of those who fatten at the public mill,
Is the chained dog beside his master's door,
Or Circe's victim, feeding on all four!

"Give me the heroes who, at tuck of drum,
Salute thy staff, immortal Quattlebum!
Or they who, doubly armed with vote and gun,
Following thy lead, illustrious Atchison,
Their drunken franchise shift from scene to scene,
As tile-beard Jourdan did his guillotine!
Rather than him who, born beneath our skies,
To Slavery's hand its supplest tool supplies;
The party felon whose unblushing face
Looks from the pillory of his bribe of place,
And coolly makes a merit of disgrace,
Points to the footmarks of indignant scorn,
Shows the deep scars of satire's tossing horn;
And passes to his credit side the sum
Of all that makes a scoundrel's martyrdom!

"Bane of the North, its canker and its moth!
These modern Esaus, bartering rights for broth!
Taxing our justice, with their double claim,
As fools for pity, and as knaves for blame;
Who, urged by party, sect, or trade, within
The fell embrace of Slavery's sphere of sin,
Part at the outset with their moral sense,
The watchful angel set for Truth's defence;
Confound all contrasts, good and ill; reverse
The poles of life, its blessing and its curse;
And lose thenceforth from their perverted sight
The eternal difference 'twixt the wrong and right;
To them the Law is but the iron span
That girds the ankles of imbruted man;
To them the Gospel has no higher aim
Than simple sanction of the master's claim,
Dragged in the slime of Slavery's loathsome trail,
Like Chalier's Bible at his ass's tail!

"Such are the men who, with instinctive dread,
Whenever Freedom lifts her drooping head,
Make prophet-tripods of their office-stools,
And scare the nurseries and the village schools
With dire presage of ruin grim and great,
A broken Union and a foundered State!
Such are the patriots, self-bound to the stake

Of office, martyrs for their country's sake:
Who fill themselves the hungry jaws of Fate,
And by their loss of manhood save the State.
In the wide gulf themselves like Curtius throw,
And test the virtues of cohesive dough;
As tropic monkeys, linking heads and tails,
Bridge o'er some torrent of Ecuador's vales!

    "Such are the men who in your churches rave
To swearing-point, at mention of the slave!
When some poor parson, haply unawares,
Stammers of freedom in his timid prayers;
Who, if some foot-sore negro through the town
Steals northward, volunteer to hunt him down.
Or, if some neighbor, flying from disease,
Courts the mild balsam of the Southern breeze,
With hue and cry pursue him on his track,
And write *Free-soiler* on the poor man's back.
Such are the men who leave the pedler's cart,
While faring South, to learn the driver's art,
Or, in white neckcloth, soothe with pious aim
The graceful sorrows of some languid dame,
Who, from the wreck of her bereavement, saves
The double charm of widowhood and slaves!
Pliant and apt, they lose no chance to show
To what base depths apostasy can go;
Outdo the natives in their readiness
To roast a negro, or to mob a press;
Poise a tarred schoolmate on the lyncher's rail,
Or make a bonfire of their birthplace mail!

    "So some poor wretch, whose lips no longer bear
The sacred burden of his mother's prayer,
By fear impelled, or lust of gold enticed,
Turns to the Crescent from the Cross of Christ,
And, over-acting in superfluous zeal,
Crawls prostrate where the faithful only kneel,
Out-howls the Dervish, hugs his rags to court
The squalid Santon's sanctity of dirt;
And, when beneath the city gateway's span
Files slow and long the Meccan caravan,
And through its midst, pursued by Islam's prayers,

The prophet's Word some favored camel bears,
The marked apostate has his place assigned
The Koran-bearer's sacred rump behind,
With brush and pitcher following, grave and mute,
In meek attendance on the holy brute!

"Men of the North! beneath your very eyes,
By hearth and home, your real danger lies.
Still day by day some hold of freedom falls
Through home-bred traitors fed within its walls.
Men whom yourselves with vote and purse sustain,
At posts of honor, influence, and gain;
The right of Slavery to your sons to teach,
And 'South-side' Gospels in your pulpits preach,
Transfix the Law to ancient freedom dear
On the sharp point of her subverted spear,
And imitate upon her cushion plump
The mad Missourian lynching from his stump;
Or, in your name, upon the Senate's floor
Yield up to Slavery all it asks, and more;
And, ere your dull eyes open to the cheat,
Sell your old homestead underneath your feet!
While such as these your loftiest outlooks hold,
While truth and conscience with your wares
        are sold,
While grave-browed merchants band themselves
        to aid
An annual man-hunt for their Southern trade,
What moral power within your grasp remains
To stay the mischief on Nebraska's plains?
High as the tides of generous impulse flow,
As far rolls back the selfish undertow;
And all your brave resolves, though aimed as true
As the horse-pistol Balmawhapple drew,
To Slavery's bastions lend as slight a shock
As the poor trooper's shot to Stirling rock!

"Yet, while the need of Freedom's cause demands
The earnest efforts of your hearts and hands,
Urged by all motives that can prompt the heart
To prayer and toil and manhood's manliest part;
Though to the soul's deep tocsin Nature joins

110

The warning whisper of her Orphic pines,
The north-wind's anger, and the south-wind's sigh,
The midnight sword-dance of the northern sky,
And, to the ear that bends above the sod
Of the green grave-mounds in the Fields of God,
In low, deep murmurs of rebuke or cheer,
The land's dead fathers speak their hope or fear,
Yet let not Passion wrest from Reason's hand
The guiding rein and symbol of command.
Blame not the caution proffering to your zeal
A well-meant drag upon its hurrying wheel;
Nor chide the man whose honest doubt extends
To the means only, not the righteous ends;
Nor fail to weigh the scruples and the fears
Of milder natures and serener years.
In the long strife with evil which began
With the first lapse of new-created man,
Wisely and well has Providence assigned
To each his part, — some forward, some behind;
And they, too, serve who temper and restrain
The o'erwarm heart that sets on fire the brain.
True to yourselves, feed Freedom's altar-flame
With what you have; let others do the same.
Spare timid doubters; set like flint your face
Against the self-sold knaves of gain and place:
Pity the weak; but with unsparing hand
Cast out the traitors who infest the land;
From bar, press, pulpit, cast them everywhere,
By dint of fasting, if you fail by prayer.
And in their place bring men of antique mould,
Like the grave fathers of your Age of Gold;
Statesmen like those who sought the primal fount
Of righteous law, the Sermon on the Mount;
Lawyers who prize, like Quincy, (to our day
Still spared, Heaven bless him!) honor more
        than pay,
And Christian jurists, starry-pure, like Jay;
Preachers like Woolman, or like them who bore
The faith of Wesley to our Western shore,
And held no convert genuine till he broke
Alike his servants' and the Devil's yoke;
And priests like him who Newport's market trod,

111

And o'er its slave-ships shook the bolts of God!
So shall your power, with a wise prudence used,
Strong but forbearing, firm but not abused,
In kindly keeping with the good of all,
The nobler maxims of the past recall,
Her natural home-born right to Freedom give,
And leave her foe his robber-right, — to live.
Live, as the snake does in his noisome fen!
Live, as the wolf does in his bone-strewn den!
Live, clothed with cursing like a robe of flame,
The focal point of million-fingered shame!
Live, till the Southron, who, with all his faults,
Has manly instincts, in his pride revolts,
Dashes from off him, midst the glad world's cheers,
The hideous nightmare of his dream of years,
And lifts, self-prompted, with his own right hand,
The vile encumbrance from his glorious land!

"So, wheresoe'er our destiny sends forth
Its widening circles to the South or North,
Where'er our banner flaunts beneath the stars
Its mimic splendors and its cloudlike bars,
There shall Free Labor's hardy children stand
The equal sovereigns of a slaveless land.
And when at last the hunted bison tires,
And dies o'ertaken by the squatter's fires;
And westward, wave on wave, the living flood
Breaks on the snow-line of majestic Hood;
And lonely Shasta listening hears the tread
Of Europe's fair-haired children, Hesper-led;
And, gazing downward through his hoar-locks,
sees
The tawny Asian climb his giant knees,
The Eastern sea shall hush his waves to hear
Pacific's surf-beat answer Freedom's cheer,
And one long rolling fire of triumph run
Between the sunrise and the sunset gun!"

❧ ☙

My task is done. The Showman and his show,
Themselves but shadows, into shadows go;

And, if no song of idlesse I have sung,
Nor tints of beauty on the canvas flung;
If the harsh numbers grate on tender ears,
And the rough picture overwrought appears;
With deeper coloring, with a sterner blast,
Before my soul a voice and vision passed,
Such as might Milton's jarring trump require,
Or glooms of Dante fringed with lurid fire.
Oh, not of choice, for themes of public wrong
I leave the green and pleasant paths of song,
The mild, sweet words which soften and adorn,
For sharp rebuke and bitter laugh of scorn.
More dear to me some song of private worth,
Some homely idyl of my native North,
Some summer pastoral of her inland vales,
Or, grim and weird, her winter fireside tales
Haunted by ghosts of unreturning sails,
Lost barks at parting hung from stem to helm
With prayers of love like dreams on Virgil's elm.
Nor private grief nor malice holds my pen;
I owe but kindness to my fellow-men;
And, South or North, wherever hearts of prayer
Their woes and weakness to our Father bear,
Wherever fruits of Christian love are found
In holy lives, to me is holy ground.
But the time passes. It were vain to crave
A late indulgence. What I had I gave.
Forget the poet, but his warning heed,
And shame his poor word with your nobler deed.

1856.

Mary Garvin

From the heart of Waumbek Methna, from the
    lake that never fails,
Falls the Saco in the green lap of Conway's intervales;
There, in wild and virgin freshness, its waters
    foam and flow,
As when Darby Field first saw them, two hundred
    years ago.

But, vexed in all its seaward course with bridges,
    dams, and mills,
How changed is Saco's stream, how lost its
    freedom of the hills,
Since travelled Jocelyn, factor Vines, and stately
    Champernoon
Heard on its banks the gray wolf's howl, the
    trumpet of the loon!

With smoking axle hot with speed, with steeds
    of fire and steam,
Wide-waked To-day leaves Yesterday behind him
    like a dream.
Still, from the hurrying train of Life, fly backward
    far and fast
The milestones of the fathers, the landmarks
    of the past.

But human hearts remain unchanged: the sorrow
    and the sin,
The loves and hopes and fears of old, are to
    our own akin;
And if, in tales our fathers told, the songs our
    mothers sung,
Tradition wears a snowy beard, Romance is always
    young.

O sharp-lined man of traffic, on Saco's banks
    to-day!
O mill-girl watching late and long the shuttle's
    restless play!
Let, for the once, a listening ear the working hand
    beguile,
And lend my old Provincial tale, as suits, a tear
    or smile!

The evening gun had sounded from gray Fort
    Mary's walls;
Through the forest, like a wild beast, roared and
    plunged the Saco's falls.

And westward on the sea-wind, that damp and
    gusty grew,
Over cedars darkening inland the smokes of
    Spurwink blew.

On the hearth of Farmer Garvin, blazed the crack-
    ling walnut log;
Right and left sat dame and goodman, and between
    them lay the dog,

Head on paws, and tail slow wagging, and beside
    him on her mat,
Sitting drowsy in the firelight, winked and purred
    the mottled cat.

"Twenty years!" said Goodman Garvin, speaking
    sadly, under breath,
And his gray head slowly shaking, as one who
    speaks of death.

The goodwife dropped her needles: "It is twenty
    years to-day,
Since the Indians fell on Saco, and stole our
    child away."

Then they sank into the silence, for each knew
    the other's thought,

115

Of a great and common sorrow, and words were
    needed not.

"Who knocks?" cried Goodman Garvin. The
    door was open thrown;
On two strangers, man and maiden, cloaked and
    furred, the fire-light shone.

One with courteous gesture lifted the bear-skin
    from his head;
"Lives here Elkanah Garvin?" "I am he," the
    goodman said.

"Sit ye down, and dry and warm ye, for the night
    is chill with rain."
And the goodwife drew the settle, and stirred the
    fire amain.

The maid unclasped her cloak-hood, the firelight
    glistened fair
In her large, moist eyes, and over soft folds
    of dark brown hair.

Dame Garvin looked upon her: "It is Mary's self
    I see!
Dear heart!" she cried, "now tell me, has my
    child come back to me?"

"My name indeed is Mary," said the stranger
    sobbing wild;
"Will you be to me a mother? I am Mary
    Garvin's child!

"She sleeps by wooded Simcoe, but on her dying
    day
She bade my father take me to her kinsfolk far
    away.

"And when the priest besought her to do me
    no such wrong,
She said, 'May God forgive me! I have closed
    my heart too long.

" 'When I hid me from my father, and shut out
        my mother's call,
    I sinned against those dear ones, and the Father
        of us all.

" 'Christ's love rebukes no home-love, breaks no
        tie of kin apart;
    Better heresy in doctrine, than heresy of heart.

" 'Tell me not the Church must censure: she who
        wept the Cross beside
    Never made her own flesh strangers, nor the claims
        of blood denied;

" 'And if she who wronged her parents, with her
        child atones to them,
    Earthly daughter, Heavenly Mother! thou at least
        wilt not condemn!'

  "So, upon her death-bed lying, my blessed mother
        spake;
    As we come to do her bidding, so receive us for
        her sake."

  "God be praised!" said Goodwife Garvin, "He
        taketh, and He gives;
    He woundeth, but He healeth; in her child our
        daughter lives!"

  "Amen!" the old man answered, as he brushed
        a tear away,
    And, kneeling by his hearthstone, said, with reverence,
        "Let us pray."

  All its Oriental symbols, and its Hebrew
        paraphrase,
    Warm with earnest life and feeling, rose his prayer
        of love and praise.

  But he started at beholding, as he rose from off
        his knee,

The stranger cross his forehead with the sign
    of Papistrie.

"What is this?" cried Farmer Garvin. "Is an
    English Christian's home
A chapel or a mass-house, that you make the sign
    of Rome?"

Then the young girl knelt beside him, kissed his
    trembling hand, and cried:
"Oh, forbear to chide my father; in that faith
    my mother died!

"On her wooden cross at Simcoe the dews and
    sunshine fall,
As they fall on Spurwink's graveyard; and the
    dear God watches all!"

The old man stroked the fair head that rested on
    his knee;
"Your words, dear child," he answered, "are God's
    rebuke to me.

"Creed and rite perchance may differ, yet our
    faith and hope be one.
Let me be your father's father, let him be
    to me a son."

When the horn, on Sabbath morning, through the
    still and frosty air,
From Spurwink, Pool, and Black Point, called to
    sermon and to prayer,

To the goodly house of worship, where, in order
    due and fit,
As by public vote directed, classed and ranked
    the people sit;

Mistress first and goodwife after, clerkly squire
    before the clown,
From the brave coat, lace-embroidered, to the gray
    frock, shading down;

From the pulpit read the preacher, "Goodman
      Garvin and his wife
Fain would thank the Lord, whose kindness has
      followed them through life,

"For the great and crowning mercy, that their
      daughter, from the wild,
Where she rests (they hope in God's peace), has
      sent to them her child;

"And the prayers of all God's people they ask,
      that they may prove
Not unworthy, through their weakness, of such
      special proof of love."

As the preacher prayed, uprising, the aged couple
      stood,
And the fair Canadian also, in her modest maidenhood.

Thought the elders, grave and doubting, "She is
      Papist born and bred;"
Thought the young men, " 'T is an angel in Mary
      Garvin's stead!"

     1856.

The Last Walk
in Autumn

I.

O'er the bare woods, whose outstretched hands
    Plead with the leaden heavens in vain,
I see, beyond the valley lands,
    The sea's long level dim with rain.
Around me all things, stark and dumb,
Seem praying for the snows to come,
And, for the summer bloom and greenness gone,
With winter's sunset lights and dazzling morn
        atone.

II.

Along the river's summer walk,
    The withered tufts of asters nod;
And trembles on its arid stalk
    The hoar plume of the golden-rod.
And on a ground of sombre fir,
And azure-studded juniper,
The silver birch its buds of purple shows,
And scarlet berries tell where bloomed the sweet
        wild-rose!

III.

With mingled sound of horns and bells,
    A far-heard clang, the wild geese fly,
Storm-sent, from Arctic moors and fells,
    Like a great arrow through the sky,
Two dusky lines converged in one,
Chasing the southward-flying sun;
While the brave snow-bird and the hardy jay
Call to them from the pines, as if to bid them
        stay.

IV.

I passed this way a year ago:
    The wind blew south; the noon of day
Was warm as June's; and save that snow
    Flecked the low mountains far away,

And that the vernal-seeming breeze
　Mocked faded grass and leafless trees,
I might have dreamed of summer as I lay,
Watching the fallen leaves with the soft wind
　　　at play.

v.

Since then, the winter blasts have piled
　The white pagodas of the snow
On these rough slopes, and, strong and wild,
　Yon river, in its overflow
Of spring-time rain and sun, set free,
　Crashed with its ices to the sea;
And over these gray fields, then green and gold,
The summer corn has waved, the thunder's organ
　　　rolled.

vi.

Rich gift of God! A year of time!
　What pomp of rise and shut of day,
What hues wherewith our Northern clime
　Makes autumn's dropping woodlands gay,
What airs outblown from ferny dells,
　And clover-bloom and sweetbrier smells,
What songs of brooks and birds, what fruits and
　　　flowers,
Green woods and moonlit snows, have in its round
　　　been ours!

vii.

I know not how, in other lands,
　The changing seasons come and go;
What splendors fall on Syrian sands,
　What purple lights on Alpine snow!
Nor how the pomp of sunrise waits
　On Venice at her watery gates;
A dream alone to me is Arno's vale,
And the Alhambra's halls are but a traveller's tale.

viii.

Yet, on life's current, he who drifts
　Is one with him who rows or sails;
And he who wanders widest lifts

No more of beauty's jealous veils
Than he who from his doorway sees
The miracle of flowers and trees,
Feels the warm Orient in the noonday air,
And from cloud minarets hears the sunset call to
     prayer!

IX.

The eye may well be glad that looks
    Where Pharpar's fountains rise and fall;
But he who sees his native brooks
    Laugh in the sun, has seen them all.
The marble palaces of Ind
Rise round him in the snow and wind;
From his lone sweetbrier Persian Hafiz smiles,
And Rome's cathedral awe is in his woodland
     aisles.

X.

And thus it is my fancy blends
    The near at hand and far and rare;
And while the same horizon bends
    Above the silver-sprinkled hair
Which flashed the light of morning skies
On childhood's wonder-lifted eyes,
Within its round of sea and sky and field,
Earth wheels with all her zones, the Kosmos
     stands revealed.

XI.

And thus the sick man on his bed,
    The toiler to his task-work bound,
Behold their prison-walls outspread,
    Their clipped horizon widen round!
While freedom-giving fancy waits,
Like Peter's angel at the gates,
The power is theirs to baffle care and pain,
To bring the lost world back, and make it theirs
     again!

XII.

What lack of goodly company,
    When masters of the ancient lyre

Obey my call, and trace for me
    Their words of mingled tears and fire!
I talk with Bacon, grave and wise,
I read the world with Pascal's eyes;
And priest and sage, with solemn brows austere,
And poets, garland-bound, the Lords of Thought,
        draw near.

XIII.

Methinks, O friend, I hear thee say,
    "In vain the human heart we mock;
Bring living guests who love the day,
    Not ghosts who fly at crow of cock!
The herbs we share with flesh and blood
Are better than ambrosial food
With laurelled shade." I grant it, nothing
        loath,
But doubly blest is he who can partake of both.

XIV.

He who might Plato's banquet grace,
    Have I not seen before me sit,
And watched his puritanic face,
    With more than Eastern wisdom lit?
Shrewd mystic! who, upon the back
Of his Poor Richard's Almanac,
Writing the Sufi's song, the Gentoo's dream,
Links Manu's age of thought to Fulton's age
        of steam!

XV.

Here too, of answering love secure,
    Have I not welcomed to my hearth
The gentle pilgrim troubadour,
    Whose songs have girdled half the earth;
Whose pages, like the magic mat
Whereon the Eastern lover sat,
Have borne me over Rhine-land's purple vines,
And Nubia's tawny sands, and Phrygia's mountain
        pines!

XVI

And he, who to the lettered wealth
    Of ages adds the lore unpriced,
The wisdom and the moral health,
    The ethics of the school of Christ;
The statesman to his holy trust,
    As the Athenian archon, just,
Struck down, exiled like him for truth alone,
Has he not graced my home with beauty all
        his own?

XVII.

What greetings smile, what farewells wave,
    What loved ones enter and depart!
The good, the beautiful, the brave,
    The Heaven-lent treasures of the heart!
How conscious seems the frozen sod
And beechen slope whereon they trod!
The oak-leaves rustle, and the dry grass
        bends
Beneath the shadowy feet of lost or absent
        friends.

XVIII.

Then ask not why to these bleak hills
    I cling, as clings the tufted moss,
To bear the winter's lingering chills,
    The mocking spring's perpetual loss.
I dream of lands where summer smiles,
And soft winds blow from spicy isles,
But scarce would Ceylon's breath of flowers
        be sweet,
Could I not feel thy soil, New England, at
        my feet!

XIX.

At times I long for gentler skies,
    And bathe in dreams of softer air,
But homesick tears would fill the eyes
    That saw the Cross without the Bear.
The pine must whisper to the palm,
The north-wind break the tropic calm;
And with the dreamy languor of the Line,

The North's keen virtue blend, and strength to
　　beauty join.

XX

Better to stem with heart and hand
　　The roaring tide of life, than lie,
Unmindful, on its flowery strand,
　　Of God's occasions drifting by!
Better with naked nerve to bear
The needles of this goading air,
Than, in the lap of sensual ease, forego
The godlike power to do, the godlike aim to know.

XXI.

Home of my heart! to me more fair
　　Than gay Versailles or Windsor's halls,
The painted, shingly town-house where
　　The freeman's vote for Freedom falls!
The simple roof where prayer is made,
Than Gothic groin and colonnade;
The living temple of the heart of man,
Than Rome's sky-mocking vault, or many-spired
　　Milan!

XXII.

More dear thy equal village schools,
　　Where rich and poor the Bible read,
Than classic halls where Priestcraft rules,
　　And Learning wears the chains of Creed;
Thy glad Thanksgiving, gathering in
The scattered sheaves of home and kin,
Than the mad license ushering Lenten pains,
Or holidays of slaves who laugh and dance
　　in chains.

XXIII.

And sweet homes nestle in these dales,
　　And perch along these wooded swells;
And, blest beyond Arcadian vales,
　　They hear the sound of Sabbath bells!
Here dwells no perfect man sublime,
Nor woman winged before her time,
But with the faults and follies of the race,

Old home-bred virtues hold their not
    unhonored place.

XXIV.

Here manhood struggles for the sake
    Of mother, sister, daughter, wife,
The graces and the loves which make
    The music of the march of life;
And woman, in her daily round
Of duty, walks on holy ground.
No unpaid menial tills the soil, nor here
Is the bad lesson learned at human rights
    to sneer.

XXV.

Then let the icy north-wind blow
    The trumpets of the coming storm,
To arrowy sleet and blinding snow
    Yon slanting lines of rain transform.
Young hearts shall hail the drifted cold,
As gayly as I did of old;
And I, who watch them through the frosty
    pane,
Unenvious, live in them my boyhood o'er again.

XXVI.

And I will trust that He who heeds
    The life that hides in mead and wold,
Who hangs yon alder's crimson beads,
    And stains these mosses green and gold,
Will still, as He hath done, incline
His gracious care to me and mine;
Grant what we ask aright, from wrong debar,
And, as the earth grows dark, make brighter
    every star!

XXVII.

I have not seen, I may not see,
    My hopes for man take form in fact,
But God will give the victory
    In due time; in that faith I act.
And he who sees the future sure,

126

The baffling present may endure,
And bless, meanwhile, the unseen Hand that
        leads
The heart's desires beyond the halting step of
        deeds.

XXVIII.

And thou, my song, I send thee forth,
    Where harsher songs of mine have flown;
Go, find a place at home and hearth
    Where'er thy singer's name is known;
Revive for him the kindly thought
Of friends; and they who love him not,
Touched by some strain of thine, perchance may
        take
The hand he proffers all, and thank him for
        thy sake.

1857.

The Garrison
of Cape Ann

From the hills of home forth looking, far beneath
    the tent-like span
Of the sky, I see the white gleam of the headland
    of Cape Ann.
Well I know its coves and beaches to the ebb-tide
    glimmering down,
And the white-walled hamlet children of its ancient
    fishing-town.

Long has passed the summer morning, and its
    memory waxes old,
When along yon breezy headlands with a pleasant
    friend I strolled.
Ah! the autumn sun is shining, and the ocean
    wind blows cool,
And the golden-rod and aster bloom around thy
    grave, Rantoul!

With the memory of that morning by the summer
    sea I blend
A wild and wondrous story, by the younger Mather
    penned,
In that quaint *Magnalia Christi*, with all strange
    and marvellous things,
Heaped up huge and undigested, like the chaos
    Ovid sings.

Dear to me these far, faint glimpses of the dual
    life of old,
Inward, grand with awe and reverence; outward,
    mean and coarse and cold;

Gleams of mystic beauty playing over dull and
    vulgar clay,
Golden-threaded fancies weaving in a web of
    hodden gray.

The great eventful Present hides the Past; but
    through the din
Of its loud life hints and echoes from the life
    behind steal in;
And the lore of home and fireside, and the legendary
    rhyme,
Make the task of duty lighter which the true man
    owes his time.

So, with something of the feeling which the
    Covenanter knew,
When with pious chisel wandering Scotland's
    moorland graveyards through,
From the graves of old traditions I part the
    blackberry-vines,
Wipe the moss from off the headstones, and
    retouch the faded lines.

❧ ☙

Where the sea-waves back and forward, hoarse
    with rolling pebbles, ran,
The garrison-house stood watching on the gray
    rocks of Cape Ann;
On its windy site uplifting gabled roof and
    palisade,
And rough walls of unhewn timber with the moon-
    light overlaid.

On his slow round walked the sentry, south and
    eastward looking forth
O'er a rude and broken coast-line, white with
    breakers stretching north, —
Wood and rock and gleaming sand-drift, jagged
    capes, with bush and tree,
Leaning inland from the smiting of the wild
    and gusty sea.

Before the deep-mouthed chimney, dimly lit
    by dying brands,
Twenty soldiers sat and waited, with their muskets
    in their hands;
On the rough-hewn oaken table the venison haunch
    was shared,
And the pewter tankard circled slowly round from
    beard to beard.

Long they sat and talked together, — talked of
    wizards Satan-sold;
Of all ghostly sights and noises, — signs and
    wonders manifold;
Of the spectre-ship of Salem, with the dead men
    in her shrouds,
Sailing sheer above the water, in the loom of
    morning clouds;

Of the marvellous valley hidden in the depths of
    Gloucester woods,
Full of plants that love the summer, — blooms
    of warmer latitudes;
Where the Arctic birch is braided by the tropic's
    flowery vines,
And the white magnolia-blossoms star the twilight
    of the pines!

But their voices sank yet lower, sank to husky
    tones of fear,
As they spake of present tokens of the powers
    of evil near;
Of a spectral host, defying stroke of steel and aim
    of gun;
Never yet was ball to slay them in the mould
    of mortals run!

Thrice, with plumes and flowing scalp-locks, from
    the midnight wood they came, —
Thrice around the block-house marching, met,
    unharmed, its volleyed flame;
Then, with mocking laugh and gesture, sunk in
    earth or lost in air,

All the ghostly wonder vanished, and the moonlit
    sands lay bare.

Midnight came; from out the forest moved
    a dusky mass that soon
Grew to warriors, plumed and painted, grimly
    marching in the moon.
"Ghosts or witches," said the captain, "thus I foil
    the Evil One!"
And he rammed a silver button, from his doublet,
    down his gun.

Once again the spectral horror moved the guarded
    wall about;
Once again the levelled muskets through the
    palisades flashed out,
With that deadly aim the squirrel on his tree-top
    might not shun,
Nor the beach-bird seaward flying with his slant
    wing to the sun.

Like the idle rain of summer sped the harmless
    shower of lead.
With a laugh of fierce derision, once again
    the phantoms fled;
Once again, without a shadow on the sands the
    moonlight lay,
And the white smoke curling through it drifted
    slowly down the bay!

"God preserve us!" said the captain; "never
    mortal foes were there;
They have vanished with their leader, Prince and
    Power of the air!
Lay aside your useless weapons; skill and prowess
    naught avail;
They who do the Devil's service wear their
    master's coat of mail!"

So the night grew near to cock-crow, when again
    a warning call

Roused the score of weary soldiers watching round
    the dusky hall:
And they looked to flint and priming, and they
    longed for break of day;
But the captain closed his Bible: "Let us cease
    from man, and pray!"

To the men who went before us, all the unseen
    powers seemed near,
And their steadfast strength of courage struck
    its roots in holy fear.
Every hand forsook the musket, every head was
    bowed and bare,
Every stout knee pressed the flag-stones, as the
    captain led in prayer.

Ceased thereat the mystic marching of the spectres
    round the wall,
But a sound abhorred, unearthly, smote the ears
    and hearts of all, —
Howls of rage and shrieks of anguish! Never
    after mortal man
Saw the ghostly leaguers marching round the
    block-house of Cape Ann.

So to us who walk in summer through the cool
    and sea-blown town,
From the childhood of its people comes the solemn
    legend down.
Not in vain the ancient fiction, in whose moral
    lives the youth
And the fitness and the freshness of an undecaying
    truth.

Soon or late to all our dwellings come the spectres
    of the mind.
Doubts and fears and dread forebodings, in
    the darkness undefined;
Round us throng the grim projections of the heart
    and of the brain,

And our pride of strength is weakness, and the
    cunning hand is vain.

In the dark we cry like children; and no answer
    from on high
Breaks the crystal spheres of silence, and no white
    wings downward fly;
But the heavenly help we pray for comes to faith,
    and not to sight,
And our prayers themselves drive backward all
    the spirits of the night!

1857.

Skipper Ireson's Ride

In the valuable and carefully prepared *History of Marblehead*, published in 1879 by Samuel Roads, Jr., it is stated that the crew of Captain Ireson, rather than himself, were responsible for the abandonment of the disabled vessel. To screen themselves they charged their captain with the crime. In view of this the writer of the ballad addressed the following letter to the historian: —

OAK KNOLL, DANVERS, 5 *mo.* 18, 1880.

MY DEAR FRIEND: I heartily thank thee for a copy of thy *History of Marblehead*. I have read it with great interest and think good use has been made of the abundant material. No town in Essex County has a record more honorable than Marblehead; no one has done more to develop the industrial interests of our New England seaboard, and certainly none have given such evidence of self-sacrificing patriotism. I am glad the story of it has been at last told, and told so well. I have now no doubt that thy version of Skipper Ireson's ride is the correct one. My verse was founded solely on a fragment of rhyme which I heard from one of my early schoolmates, a native of Marblehead.

I supposed the story to which it referred dated back at least a century. I knew nothing of the participators, and the narrative of the ballad was pure fancy. I am glad for the sake of truth and justice that the real facts are given in thy book. I certainly would not knowingly do injustice to any one, dead or living.

I am very truly thy friend,

JOHN G. WHITTIER.

Of all the rides since the birth of time,
Told in story or sung in rhyme, —
On Apuleius's Golden Ass,
Or one-eyed Calendar's horse of brass,
Witch astride of a human back,
Islam's prophet on Al-Borák, —
The strangest ride that ever was sped
Was Ireson's, out from Marblehead!
    Old Floyd Ireson, for his hard heart,
        Tarred and feathered and carried in a cart
            By the women of Marblehead!

Body of turkey, head of owl,
Wings a-droop like a rained-on fowl,
Feathered and ruffled in every part,
Skipper Ireson stood in the cart.
Scores of women, old and young,
Strong of muscle, and glib of tongue,
Pushed and pulled up the rocky lane,
Shouting and singing the shrill refrain:
    "Here's Flud Oirson, fur his horrd horrt,
      Torr'd an' futherr'd an' corr'd in a corrt
        By the women o' Morble'ead!"

Wrinkled scolds with hands on hips,
Girls in bloom of cheek and lips,
Wild-eyed, free-limbed, such as chase
Bacchus round some antique vase,
Brief of skirt, with ankles bare,
Loose of kerchief and loose of hair,
With conch-shells blowing and fish-horns' twang,
Over and over the Mænads sang:
    "Here's Flud Oirson, fur his horrd horrt,
      Torr'd an' futherr'd an' corr'd in a corrt
        By the women o' Morble'ead!"

Small pity for him! — He sailed away
From a leaking ship, in Chaleur Bay, —
Sailed away from a sinking wreck,
With his own town's-people on her deck!
"Lay by! lay by!" they called to him.
Back he answered, "Sink or swim!
Brag of your catch of fish again!"
And off he sailed through the fog and rain!
    Old Floyd Ireson, for his hard heart,
      Tarred and feathered and carried in a cart
        By the women of Marblehead!

Fathoms deep in dark Chaleur
That wreck shall lie forevermore.
Mother and sister, wife and maid,
Looked from the rocks of Marblehead
Over the moaning and rainy sea, —
Looked for the coming that might not be!

What did the winds and the sea-birds say
Of the cruel captain who sailed away? —
  Old Floyd Ireson, for his hard heart,
  Tarred and feathered and carried in a cart
    By the women of Marblehead!

Through the street, on either side,
Up flew windows, doors swung wide;
Sharp-tongued spinsters, old wives gray,
Treble lent the fish-horn's bray.
Sea-worn grandsires, cripple-bound,
Hulks of old sailors run aground,
Shook head, and fist, and hat, and came,
And cracked with curses the hoarse refrain:
  "Here's Flud Oirson, fur his horrd horrt,
  Torr'd an' futherr'd an' corr'd in a corrt
    By the women o' Morble'ead!"

Sweetly along the Salem road
Bloom of orchard and lilac showed.
Little the wicked skipper knew
Of the fields so green and the sky so blue.
Riding there in his sorry trim,
Like an Indian idol glum and grim,
Scarcely he seemed the sound to hear
Of voices shouting, far and near:
  "Here's Flud Oirson, fur his horrd horrt,
  Torr'd an' futherr'd an' corr'd in a corrt
    By the women o' Morble'ead!"

"Hear me, neighbors!" at last he cried, —
"What to me is this noisy ride?
What is the shame that clothes the skin
To the nameless horror that lives within?
Waking or sleeping, I see a wreck,
And hear a cry from a reeling deck!
Hate me and curse me, — I only dread
The hand of God and the face of the dead!"
  Said old Floyd Ireson, for his hard heart,
  Tarred and feathered and carried in a cart
    By the women of Marblehead!

Then the wife of the skipper lost at sea
Said, "God has touched him! why should we?"
Said an old wife mourning her only son,
"Cut the rogue's tether and let him run!"
So with soft relentings and rude excuse,
Half scorn, half pity, they cut him loose,
And gave him a cloak to hide him in,
And left him alone with his shame and sin.
 Poor Floyd Ireson, for his hard heart,
 Tarred and feathered and carried in a cart
  By the women of Marblehead!

1857.

Telling the Bees

A remarkable custom, brought from the Old Country, formerly prevailed in the rural districts of New England. On the death of a member of the family, the bees were at once informed of the event, and their hives dressed in mourning. This ceremonial was supposed to be necessary to prevent the swarms from leaving their hives and seeking a new home.

Here is the place; right over the hill
    Runs the path I took;
You can see the gap in the old wall still,
    And the stepping-stones in the shallow brook.

There is the house, with the gate red-barred,
    And the poplars tall;
And the barn's brown length, and the cattle-yard,
    And the white horns tossing above the wall.

There are the beehives ranged in the sun;
    And down by the brink
Of the brook are her poor flowers, weed-o'errun,
    Pansy and daffodil, rose and pink.

A year has gone, as the tortoise goes,
    Heavy and slow;
And the same rose blows, and the same sun glows,
    And the same brook sings of a year ago.

There's the same sweet clover-smell in the breeze;
    And the June sun warm
Tangles his wings of fire in the trees,
    Setting, as then, over Fernside farm.

I mind me how with a lover's care
    From my Sunday coat
I brushed off the burrs, and smoothed my hair,
    And cooled at the brookside my brow
        and throat.

Since we parted, a month had passed, —
    To love, a year;

Down through the beeches I looked at last
  On the little red gate and the well-sweep near.

I can see it all now, — the slantwise rain
  Of light through the leaves,
The sundown's blaze on her window-pane,
  The bloom of her roses under the eaves.

Just the same as a month before, —
  The house and the trees,
The barn's brown gable, the vine by the door, —
  Nothing changed but the hives of bees.

Before them, under the garden wall,
  Forward and back,
Went drearily singing the chore-girl small,
  Draping each hive with a shred of black.

Trembling, I listened: the summer sun
  Had the chill of snow;
For I knew she was telling the bees of one
  Gone on the journey we all must go!

Then I said to myself, "My Mary weeps
  For the dead to-day:
Haply her blind old grandsire sleeps
  The fret and the pain of his age away."

But her dog whined low; on the doorway sill,
  With his cane to his chin,
The old man sat; and the chore-girl still
  Sung to the bees stealing out and in.

And the song she was singing ever since
  In my ear sounds on: —
"Stay at home, pretty bees, fly not hence!
  Mistress Mary is dead and gone!"

1858.

139

The Pipes at Lucknow

An incident of the Sepoy mutiny.

Pipes of the misty moorlands,
    Voice of the glens and hills;
The droning of the torrents,
    The treble of the rills!
Not the braes of broom and heather,
    Nor the mountains dark with rain,
Nor maiden bower, nor border tower,
    Have heard your sweetest strain!

Dear to the Lowland reaper,
    And plaided mountaineer, —
To the cottage and the castle
    The Scottish pipes are dear; —
Sweet sounds the ancient pibroch
    O'er mountain, loch, and glade;
But the sweetest of all music
    The pipes at Lucknow played.

Day by day the Indian tiger
    Louder yelled, and nearer crept;
Round and round the jungle-serpent
    Near and nearer circles swept.
"Pray for rescue, wives and mothers, —
    Pray to-day!" the soldier said;
"To-morrow, death's between us
    And the wrong and shame we dread."

Oh, they listened, looked, and waited,
    Till their hope became despair;
And the sobs of low bewailing
    Filled the pauses of their prayer.

140

Then up spake a Scottish maiden,
  With her ear unto the ground:
"Dinna ye hear it? — dinna ye hear it?
  The pipes o' Havelock sound!"

Hushed the wounded man his groaning;
  Hushed the wife her little ones;
Alone they heard the drum-roll
  And the roar of Sepoy guns.
But to sounds of home and childhood
  The Highland ear was true; —
As her mother's cradle-crooning
  The mountain pipes she knew.

Like the march of soundless music
  Through the vision of the seer,
More of feeling than of hearing,
  Of the heart than of the ear,
She knew the droning pibroch,
  She knew the Campbell's call:
"Hark! hear ye no' MacGregor's,
  The grandest o' them all!"

Oh, they listened, dumb and breathless,
  And they caught the sound at last;
Faint and far beyond the Goomtee
  Rose and fell the piper's blast!
Then a burst of wild thanksgiving
  Mingled woman's voice and man's;
"God be praised! — the march of Havelock!
  The piping of the clans!"

Louder, nearer, fierce as vengeance,
  Sharp and shrill as swords at strife,
Came the wild MacGregor's clan-call,
  Stinging all the air to life.
But when the far-off dust-cloud
  To plaided legions grew,
Full tenderly and blithesomely
  The pipes of rescue blew!

Round the silver domes of Lucknow,
　　Moslem mosque and Pagan shrine,
Breathed the air to Britons dearest,
　　The air of Auld Lang Syne.
O'er the cruel roll of war-drums
　　Rose that sweet and homelike strain;
And the tartan clove the turban,
　　As the Goomtee cleaves the plain.

Dear to the corn-land reaper
　　And plaided mountaineer, —
To the cottage and the castle
　　The piper's song is dear.
Sweet sounds the Gaelic pibroch
　　O'er mountain, glen, and glade;
But the sweetest of all music
　　The Pipes at Lucknow played!

1858.

The Prophecy
of Samuel Sewall

The prose version of this prophecy is to be found in Sewall's *The New Heaven upon the New Earth*, 1697, quoted in Joshua Coffin's *History of Newbury*. Judge Sewall's father, Henry Sewall, was one of the pioneers of Newbury.

Up and down the village streets
Strange are the forms my fancy meets,
For the thoughts and things of to-day are hid,
And through the veil of a closëd lid
The ancient worthies I see again:
I hear the tap of the elder's cane,
And his awful periwig I see,
And the silver buckles of shoe and knee.
Stately and slow, with thoughtful air,
His black cap hiding his whitened hair,
Walks the Judge of the great Assize,
Samuel Sewall the good and wise.
His face with lines of firmness wrought,
He wears the look of a man unbought,
Who swears to his hurt and changes not;
Yet, touched and softened nevertheless
With the grace of Christian gentleness,
The face that a child would climb to kiss!
True and tender and brave and just,
That man might honor and woman trust.

Touching and sad, a tale is told,
Like a penitent hymn of the Psalmist old,
Of the fast which the good man lifelong kept
With a haunting sorrow that never slept,
As the circling year brought round the time
Of an error that left the sting of crime,
When he sat on the bench of the witchcraft
     courts,

With the laws of Moses and Hale's Reports,
And spake, in the name of both, the word
That gave the witch's neck to the cord,
And piled the oaken planks that pressed
The feeble life from the warlock's breast!
All the day long, from dawn to dawn,
His door was bolted, his curtain drawn;
No foot on his silent threshold trod,
No eye looked on him save that of God,
As he baffled the ghosts of the dead with charms
Of penitent tears, and prayers, and psalms,
And, with precious proofs from the sacred word
Of the boundless pity and love of the Lord,
His faith confirmed and his trust renewed
That the sin of his ignorance, sorely rued,
Might be washed away in the mingled flood
Of his human sorrow and Christ's dear blood!

 Green forever the memory be
Of the Judge of the old Theocracy,
Whom even his errors glorified,
Like a far-seen, sunlit mountain-side
By the cloudy shadows which o'er it glide!
Honor and praise to the Puritan
Who the halting step of his age outran,
And, seeing the infinite worth of man
In the priceless gift the Father gave,
In the infinite love that stooped to save,
Dared not brand his brother a slave!
"Who doth such wrong," he was wont to say,
In his own quaint, picture-loving way,
"Flings up to Heaven a hand-grenade
Which God shall cast down upon his head!"

 Widely as heaven and hell, contrast
That brave old jurist of the past
And the cunning trickster and knave of courts
Who the holy features of Truth distorts, —
Ruling as right the will of the strong,
Poverty, crime, and weakness wrong;
Wide-eared to power, to the wronged and weak
Deaf as Egypt's gods of leek;

Scoffing aside at party's nod
Order of nature and law of God;
For whose dabbled ermine respect were waste,
Reverence folly, and awe misplaced;
Justice of whom 't were vain to seek
As from Koordish robber or Syrian Sheik!
Oh, leave the wretch to his bribes and sins;
Let him rot in the web of lies he spins!
To the saintly soul of the early day,
To the Christian judge, let us turn and say:
"Praise and thanks for an honest man! —
Glory to God for the Puritan!"

I see, far southward, this quiet day,
The hills of Newbury rolling away,
With the many tints of the season gay,
Dreamily blending in autumn mist
Crimson, and gold, and amethyst.
Long and low, with dwarf trees crowned,
Plum Island lies, like a whale aground,
A stone's toss over the narrow sound.
Inland, as far as the eye can go,
The hills curve round like a bended bow;
A silver arrow from out them sprung,
I see the shine of the Quasycung;
And, round and round, over valley and hill,
Old roads winding, as old roads will,
Here to a ferry, and there to a mill;
And glimpses of chimneys and gabled eaves,
Through green elm arches and maple leaves, —
Old homesteads sacred to all that can
Gladden or sadden the heart of man,
Over whose thresholds of oak and stone
Life and Death have come and gone!
There pictured tiles in the fireplace show,
Great beams sag from the ceiling low,
The dresser glitters with polished wares,
The long clock ticks on the foot-worn stairs,
And the low, broad chimney shows the crack
By the earthquake made a century back.
Up from their midst springs the village spire
With the crest of its cock in the sun afire;

Beyond are orchards and planting lands,
And great salt marshes and glimmering sands,
And, where north and south the coast-lines run,
The blink of the sea in breeze and sun!

I see it all like a chart unrolled,
But my thoughts are full of the past and old,
I hear the tales of my boyhood told;
And the shadows and shapes of early days
Flit dimly by in the veiling haze,
With measured movement and rhythmic chime
Weaving like shuttles my web of rhyme.
I think of the old man wise and good
Who once on yon misty hillsides stood,
(A poet who never measured rhyme,
A seer unknown to his dull-eared time,)
And, propped on his staff of age, looked down,
With his boyhood's love, on his native town,
Where, written, as if on its hills and plains,
His burden of prophecy yet remains,
For the voices of wood, and wave, and wind
To read in the ear of the musing mind: —

"As long as Plum Island, to guard the coast
As God appointed, shall keep its post;
As long as a salmon shall haunt the deep
Of Merrimac River, or sturgeon leap;
As long as pickerel swift and slim,
Or red-backed perch, in Crane Pond swim;
As long as the annual sea-fowl know
Their time to come and their time to go;
As long as cattle shall roam at will
The green, grass meadows by Turkey Hill;
As long as sheep shall look from the side
Of Oldtown Hill on marishes wide,
And Parker River, and salt-sea tide;
As long as a wandering pigeon shall search
The fields below from his white-oak perch,
When the barley-harvest is ripe and shorn,
And the dry husks fall from the standing corn;
As long as Nature shall not grow old,
Nor drop her work from her doting hold,

And her care for the Indian corn forget,
And the yellow rows in pairs to set; —
So long shall Christians here be born,
Grow up and ripen as God's sweet corn! —
By the beak of bird, by the breath of frost,
Shall never a holy ear be lost,
But, husked by Death in the Planter's sight,
Be sown again in the fields of light!"

The Island still is purple with plums,
Up the river the salmon comes,
The sturgeon leaps, and the wild-fowl feeds
On hillside berries and marish seeds, —
All the beautiful signs remain,
From spring-time sowing to autumn rain
The good man's vision returns again!
And let us hope, as well we can,
That the Silent Angel who garners man
May find some grain as of old he found
In the human cornfield ripe and sound,
And the Lord of the Harvest deign to own
The precious seed by the fathers sown!

1859.

The Double-Headed Snake
of Newbury

"Concerning yᵉ Amphisbæna, as soon as I received your commands, I made diligent inquiry: . . . he assures me yᵗ it had really two heads, one at each end; two mouths, two stings or tongues." — REV. CHRISTO-PHER TOPPAN *to* COTTON MATHER.

Far away in the twilight time
Of every people, in every clime,
Dragons and griffins and monsters dire,
Born of water, and air, and fire,
Or nursed, like the Python, in the mud
And ooze of the old Deucalion flood,
Crawl and wriggle and foam with rage,
Through dusk tradition and ballad age.
So from the childhood of Newbury town
And its time of fable the tale comes down
Of a terror which haunted bush and brake,
The Amphisbæna, the Double Snake!

Thou who makest the tale thy mirth,
Consider that strip of Christian earth
On the desolate shore of a sailless sea,
Full of terror and mystery,
Half redeemed from the evil hold
Of the wood so dreary, and dark, and old,
Which drank with its lips of leaves the dew
When Time was young, and the world was new,
And wove its shadows with sun and moon,
Ere the stones of Cheops were squared and hewn.
Think of the sea's dread monotone,
Of the mournful wail from the pine-wood blown,
Of the strange, vast splendors that lit the North,
Of the troubled throes of the quaking earth,
And the dismal tales the Indian told,

148

Till the settler's heart at his hearth grew cold,
And he shrank from the tawny wizard boasts,
And the hovering shadows seemed full of ghosts,
And above, below, and on every side,
The fear of his creed seemed verified; —
And think, if his lot were now thine own,
To grope with terrors nor named nor known,
How laxer muscle and weaker nerve
And a feebler faith thy need might serve;
And own to thyself the wonder more
That the snake had two heads, and not a score!

Whether he lurked in the Oldtown fen
Or the gray earth-flax of the Devil's Den,
Or swam in the wooded Artichoke,
Or coiled by the Northman's Written Rock,
Nothing on record is left to show;
Only the fact that he lived, we know,
And left the cast of a double head
In the scaly mask which he yearly shed.
For he carried a head where his tail should be,
And the two, of course, could never agree,
But wriggled about with main and might,
Now to the left and now to the right;
Pulling and twisting this way and that,
Neither knew what the other was at.

A snake with two heads, lurking so near!
Judge of the wonder, guess at the fear!
Think what ancient gossips might say,
Shaking their heads in their dreary way,
Between the meetings on Sabbath-day!
How urchins, searching at day's decline
The Common Pasture for sheep or kine,
The terrible double-ganger heard
In leafy rustle or whir of bird!
Think what a zest it gave to the sport,
In berry-time, of the younger sort,
As over pastures blackberry-twined,
Reuben and Dorothy lagged behind,
And closer and closer, for fear of harm,
The maiden clung to her lover's arm;

And how the spark, who was forced to stay,
By his sweetheart's fears, till the break of day,
Thanked the snake for the fond delay!

Far and wide the tale was told,
Like a snowball growing while it rolled.
The nurse hushed with it the baby's cry;
And it served, in the worthy minister's eye,
To paint the primitive serpent by.
Cotton Mather came galloping down
All the way to Newbury town,
With his eyes agog and his ears set wide,
And his marvellous inkhorn at his side;
Stirring the while in the shallow pool
Of his brains for the lore he learned at school,
To garnish the story, with here a streak
Of Latin, and there another of Greek:
And the tales he heard and the notes he took,
Behold! are they not in his Wonder-Book?

Stories, like dragons, are hard to kill.
If the snake does not, the tale runs still
In Byfield Meadows, on Pipestave Hill.
And still, whenever husband and wife
Publish the shame of their daily strife,
And, with mad cross-purpose, tug and strain
At either end of the marriage-chain,
The gossips say, with a knowing shake
Of their gray heads, "Look at the Double Snake!
One in body and two in will,
The Amphisbæna is living still!"

1859.

My Playmate

The pines were dark on Ramoth hill,
   Their song was soft and low;
The blossoms in the sweet May wind
   Were falling like the snow.

The blossoms drifted at our feet,
   The orchard birds sang clear;
The sweetest and the saddest day
   It seemed of all the year.

For, more to me than birds or flowers,
   My playmate left her home,
And took with her the laughing spring,
   The music and the bloom.

She kissed the lips of kith and kin,
   She laid her hand in mine:
What more could ask the bashful boy
   Who fed her father's kine?

She left us in the bloom of May:
   The constant years told o'er
Their seasons with as sweet May morns,
   But she came back no more.

I walk, with noiseless feet, the round
   Of uneventful years;
Still o'er and o'er I sow the spring
   And reap the autumn ears.

She lives where all the golden year
   Her summer roses blow;

The dusky children of the sun
  Before her come and go.

There haply with her jewelled hands
  She smooths her silken gown, —
No more the homespun lap wherein
  I shook the walnuts down.

The wild grapes wait us by the brook,
  The brown nuts on the hill,
And still the May-day flowers make sweet
  The woods of Follymill.

The lilies blossom in the pond,
  The bird builds in the tree,
The dark pines sing on Ramoth hill
  The slow song of the sea.

I wonder if she thinks of them,
  And how the old time seems, —
If ever the pines of Ramoth wood
  Are sounding in her dreams.

I see her face, I hear her voice;
  Does she remember mine?
And what to her is now the boy
  Who fed her father's kine?

What cares she that the orioles build
  For other eyes than ours, —
That other hands with nuts are filled,
  And other laps with flowers?

O playmate in the golden time!
  Our mossy seat is green,
Its fringing violets blossom yet,
  The old trees o'er it lean.

The winds so sweet with birch and fern
  A sweeter memory blow;

And there in spring the veeries sing
   The song of long ago.

And still the pines of Ramoth wood
   Are moaning like the sea, —
The moaning of the sea of change
   Between myself and thee!

   1860.

"Ein Feste Burg Ist Unser Gott"

Luther's Hymn.

We wait beneath the furnace-blast
  The pangs of transformation;
Not painlessly doth God recast
  And mould anew the nation.
    Hot burns the fire
    Where wrongs expire;
    Nor spares the hand
    That from the land
  Uproots the ancient evil.

The hand-breadth cloud the sages feared
  Its bloody rain is dropping;
The poison plant the fathers spared
  All else is overtopping.
    East, West, South, North,
    It curses the earth;
    All justice dies,
    And fraud and lies
  Live only in its shadow.

What gives the wheat-field blades of steel?
  What points the rebel cannon?
What sets the roaring rabble's heel
  On the old star-spangled pennon?
    What breaks the oath
    Of the men o' the South?
    What whets the knife
    For the Union's life? —
  Hark to the answer: Slavery!

Then waste no blows on lesser foes
  In strife unworthy freemen.

God lifts to-day the veil, and shows
   The features of the demon!
     O North and South,
     Its victims both,
     Can ye not cry,
   "Let slavery die!"
   And union find in freedom?

What though the cast-out spirit tear
   The nation in his going?
We who have shared the guilt must share
   The pang of his o'erthrowing!
     Whate'er the loss,
     Whate'er the cross,
     Shall they complain
     Of present pain
   Who trust in God's hereafter?

For who that leans on His right arm
   Was ever yet forsaken?
What righteous cause can suffer harm
   If He its part has taken?
     Though wild and loud,
     And dark the cloud,
     Behind its folds
     His hand upholds
   The calm sky of to-morrow!

Above the maddening cry for blood,
   Above the wild war-drumming,
Let Freedom's voice be heard, with good
   The evil overcoming.
     Give prayer and purse
     To stay the Curse
     Whose wrong we share,
     Whose shame we bear,
   Whose end shall gladden Heaven!

In vain the bells of war shall ring
   Of triumphs and revenges,
While still is spared the evil thing
   That severs and estranges.

But blest the ear
That yet shall hear
The jubilant bell
That rings the knell
Of Slavery forever!

Then let the selfish lip be dumb,
And hushed the breath of sighing;
Before the joy of peace must come
The pains of purifying.
God give us grace
Each in his place
To bear his lot,
And, murmuring not,
Endure and wait and labor!

1861.

Monadnock from Wachuset

from

Mountain Pictures

I would I were a painter, for the sake
  Of a sweet picture, and of her who led,
  A fitting guide, with reverential tread,
Into that mountain mystery. First a lake
  Tinted with sunset; next the wavy lines
    Of far receding hills; and yet more far,
  Monadnock lifting from his night of pines
    His rosy forehead to the evening star.
Beside us, purple-zoned, Wachuset laid
His head against the West, whose warm light made
    His aureole; and o'er him, sharp and clear,
Like a shaft of lightning in mid-launching stayed,
  A single level cloud-line, shone upon
  By the fierce glances of the sunken sun,
    Menaced the darkness with its golden spear!

So twilight deepened round us. Still and black
The great woods climbed the mountain at our
        back;
And on their skirts, where yet the lingering day
On the shorn greenness of the clearing lay,
    The brown old farm-house like a bird's-nest
        hung.
With home-life sounds the desert air was stirred:
The bleat of sheep along the hill we heard,
The bucket plashing in the cool, sweet well,
The pasture-bars that clattered as they fell;
Dogs barked, fowls fluttered, cattle lowed;
        the gate

Of the barn-yard creaked beneath the merry weight
   Of sun-brown children, listening, while they
      swung,
     The welcome sound of supper-call to hear;
     And down the shadowy lane, in tinklings
      clear,
   The pastoral curfew of the cow-bell rung.
Thus soothed and pleased, our backward path
      we took,
   Praising the farmer's home. He only spake,
   Looking into the sunset o'er the lake,
     Like one to whom the far-off is most near:
"Yes, most folks think it has a pleasant look;
   I love it for my good old mother's sake,
     Who lived and died here in the peace
      of God!"
   The lesson of his words we pondered o'er,
As silently we turned the eastern flank
Of the mountain, where its shadow deepest sank,
Doubling the night along our rugged road:
We felt that man was more than his abode, —
   The inward life than Nature's raiment more;
And the warm sky, the sundown-tinted hill,
   The forest and the lake, seemed dwarfed
     and dim
Before the saintly soul, whose human will
     Meekly in the Eternal footsteps trod,
Making her homely toil and household ways
An earthly echo of the song of praise
   Swelling from angel lips and harps of
     seraphim.

   1862.

Barbara Frietchie

This poem was written in strict conformity to the account of the incident as I had it from respectable and trustworthy sources. It has since been the subject of a good deal of conflicting testimony, and the story was probably incorrect in some of its details. It is admitted by all that Barbara Frietchie was no myth, but a worthy and highly esteemed gentlewoman, intensely loyal and a hater of the Slavery Rebellion, holding her Union flag sacred and keeping it with her Bible; that when the Confederates halted before her house, and entered her dooryard, she denounced them in vigorous language, shook her cane in their faces, and drove them out; and when General Burnside's troops followed close upon Jackson's, she waved her flag and cheered them. It is stated that May Quantrell, a brave and loyal lady in another part of the city, did wave her flag in sight of the Confederates. It is possible that there has been a blending of the two incidents.

Up from the meadows rich with corn,
Clear in the cool September morn,

The clustered spires of Frederick stand
Green-walled by the hills of Maryland.

Round about them orchards sweep,
Apple and peach tree fruited deep,

Fair as the garden of the Lord
To the eyes of the famished rebel horde,

On that pleasant morn of the early fall
When Lee marched over the mountain-wall;

Over the mountains winding down,
Horse and foot, into Frederick town.

Forty flags with their silver stars,
Forty flags with their crimson bars,

Flapped in the morning wind: the sun
Of noon looked down, and saw not one.

Up rose old Barbara Frietchie then,
Bowed with her fourscore years and ten;

Bravest of all in Frederick town,
She took up the flag the men hauled down;

In her attic window the staff she set,
To show that one heart was loyal yet.

Up the street came the rebel tread,
Stonewall Jackson riding ahead.

Under his slouched hat left and right
He glanced; the old flag met his sight.

"Halt!" — the dust-brown ranks stood fast.
"Fire!" — out blazed the rifle blast.

It shivered the window, pane and sash;
It rent the banner with seam and gash.

Quick, as it fell, from the broken staff
Dame Barbara snatched the silken scarf.

She leaned far out on the window-sill,
And shook it forth with a royal will.

"Shoot, if you must, this old gray head,
But spare your country's flag," she said.

A shade of sadness, a blush of shame,
Over the face of the leader came;

The nobler nature within him stirred
To life at that woman's deed and word;

"Who touches a hair of yon gray head
Dies like a dog! March on!" he said.

All day long through Frederick street
Sounded the tread of marching feet:

All day long that free flag tost
Over the heads of the rebel host.

Ever its torn folds rose and fell
On the loyal winds that loved it well;

And through the hill-gaps sunset light
Shone over it with a warm good-night.

Barbara Frietchie's work is o'er,
And the Rebel rides on his raids no more.

Honor to her! and let a tear
Fall, for her sake, on Stonewall's bier.

Over Barbara Frietchie's grave,
Flag of Freedom and Union, wave!

Peace and order and beauty draw
Round thy symbol of light and law;

And ever the stars above look down
On thy stars below in Frederick town!

1863.

The Vanishers

Sweetest of all childlike dreams
   In the simple Indian lore
Still to me the legend seems
   Of the shapes who flit before.

Flitting, passing, seen and gone,
   Never reached nor found at rest,
Baffling search, but beckoning on
   To the Sunset of the Blest.

From the clefts of mountain rocks,
   Through the dark of lowland firs,
Flash the eyes and flow the locks
   Of the mystic Vanishers!

And the fisher in his skiff,
   And the hunter on the moss,
Hear their call from cape and cliff,
   See their hands the birch-leaves toss.

Wistful, longing, through the green
   Twilight of the clustered pines,
In their faces rarely seen
   Beauty more than mortal shines.

Fringed with gold their mantles flow
   On the slopes of westering knolls;
In the wind they whisper low
   Of the Sunset Land of Souls.

Doubt who may, O friend of mine!
   Thou and I have seen them too;

On before with beck and sign
   Still they glide, and we pursue.

More than clouds of purple trail
   In the gold of setting day;
More than gleams of wing or sail
   Beckon from the sea-mist gray.

Glimpses of immortal youth,
   Gleams and glories seen and flown,
Far-heard voices sweet with truth,
   Airs from viewless Eden blown;

Beauty that eludes our grasp,
   Sweetness that transcends our taste,
Loving hands we may not clasp,
   Shining feet that mock our haste;

Gentle eyes we closed below,
   Tender voices heard once more,
Smile and call us, as they go
   On and onward, still before.

Guided thus, O friend of mine!
   Let us walk our little way,
Knowing by each beckoning sign
   That we are not quite astray.

Chase we still, with baffled feet,
   Smiling eye and waving hand,
Sought and seeker soon shall meet,
   Lost and found, in Sunset Land!

1864.

163

Laus Deo!

On hearing the bells ring on the passage of the constitutional amendment abolishing slavery. The resolution was adopted by Congress, January 31, 1865. The ratification by the requisite number of States was announced December 18, 1865.

It is done!
  Clang of bell and roar of gun
Send the tidings up and down.
    How the belfries rock and reel!
    How the great guns, peal on peal,
Fling the joy from town to town!

  Ring, O bells!
  Every stroke exulting tells
Of the burial hour of crime.
    Loud and long, that all may hear,
    Ring for every listening ear
Of Eternity and Time!

  Let us kneel:
  God's own voice is in that peal,
And this spot is holy ground.
    Lord, forgive us! What are we,
    That our eyes this glory see,
That our ears have heard the sound!

  For the Lord
  On the whirlwind is abroad;
In the earthquake He has spoken;
    He has smitten with His thunder
    The iron walls asunder,
And the gates of brass are broken!

Loud and long
Lift the old exulting song;
Sing with Miriam by the sea,
He has cast the mighty down;
Horse and rider sink and drown;
"He hath triumphed gloriously!"

Did we dare,
In our agony of prayer,
Ask for more than He has done?
When was ever His right hand
Over any time or land
Stretched as now beneath the sun?

How they pale,
Ancient myth and song and tale,
In this wonder of our days,
When the cruel rod of war
Blossoms white with righteous law,
And the wrath of man is praise!

Blotted out!
All within and all about
Shall a fresher life begin;
Freer breathe the universe
As it rolls its heavy curse
On the dead and buried sin!

It is done!
In the circuit of the sun
Shall the sound thereof go forth.
It shall bid the sad rejoice,

It shall give the dumb a voice,
It shall belt with joy the earth!

Ring and swing,
Bells of joy! On the morning's wing
Send the song of praise abroad!
With a sound of broken chains
Tell the nations that He reigns,
Who alone is Lord and God!

1865.

Snow-Bound

A Winter Idyl

To the Memory
of
The Household It Describes,
This poem is dedicated by the author.

The inmates of the family at the Whittier homestead who are referred
to in the poem were my father, mother, my brother and two sisters,
and my uncle and aunt both unmarried. In addition, there was the
district school-master who boarded with us. The "not unfeared, half-
welcome guest" was Harriet Livermore, daughter of Judge Livermore,
of New Hampshire, a young woman of fine natural ability, enthusiastic, eccentric, with slight control over her violent temper, which
sometimes made her religious profession doubtful. She was equally
ready to exhort in school-house prayer-meetings and dance in a Washington ball-room, while her father was a member of Congress. She early
embraced the doctrine of the Second Advent, and felt it her duty to
proclaim the Lord's speedy coming. With this message she crossed the
Atlantic and spent the greater part of a long life in travelling over
Europe and Asia. She lived some time with Lady Hester Stanhope, a
woman as fantastic and mentally strained as herself, on the slope of
Mt. Lebanon, but finally quarrelled with her in regard to two white
horses with red marks on their backs which suggested the idea of saddles, on which her titled hostess expected to ride into Jerusalem with
the Lord. A friend of mine found her, when quite an old woman, wandering in Syria with a tribe of Arabs, who with the Oriental notion that
madness is inspiration, accepted her as their prophetess and leader. At
the time referred to in *Snow-Bound* she was boarding at the Rocks
Village about two miles from us.

In my boyhood, in our lonely farm-house, we had scanty sources of
information; few books and only a small weekly newspaper. Our only
annual was the Almanac. Under such circumstances story-telling was
a necessary resource in the long winter evenings. My father when a
young man had traversed the wilderness to Canada, and could tell us
of his adventures with Indians and wild beasts, and of his sojourn in
the French villages. My uncle was ready with his record of hunting
and fishing and, it must be confessed, with stories which he at least
half believed, of witchcraft and apparitions. My mother, who was born
in the Indian-haunted region of Somersworth, New Hampshire, between
Dover and Portsmouth, told us of the inroads of the savages, and the

167

narrow escape of her ancestors. She described strange people who lived on the Piscataqua and Cocheco, among whom was Bantam the sorcerer. I have in my possession the wizard's "conjuring book," which he solemnly opened when consulted. It is a copy of Cornelius Agrippa's *Magic* printed in 1651, dedicated to Dr. Robert Child, who, like Michael Scott, had learned

> "the art of glammorie
> In Padua beyond the sea,"

and who is famous in the annals of Massachusetts, where he was at one time a resident, as the first man who dared petition the General Court for liberty of conscience. The full title of the book is *Three Books of Occult Philosophy, by Henry Cornelius Agrippa, Knight, Doctor of both Laws, Counsellor to Cæsar's Sacred Majesty and Judge of the Prerogative Court.*

"As the Spirits of Darkness be stronger in the dark, so Good Spirits, which be Angels of Light, are augmented not only by the Divine light of the Sun, but also by our common VVood Fire: and as the Celestial Fire drives away dark spirits, so also this our Fire of the VVood doth the same." — COR. AGRIPPA, *Occult Philosophy*, Book I. ch. v.

> "Announced by all the trumpets of the sky,
> Arrives the snow, and, driving o'er the fields,
> Seems nowhere to alight: the whited air
> Hides hills and woods, the river and the heaven,
> And veils the farm-house at the garden's end.
> The sled and traveller stopped, the courier's feet
> Delayed, all friends shut out, the housemates sit
> Around the radiant fireplace, enclosed
> In a tumultuous privacy of storm."
>
> EMERSON. *The Snow Storm.*

The sun that brief December day
Rose cheerless over hills of gray,
And, darkly circled, gave at noon
A sadder light than waning moon.
Slow tracing down the thickening sky
Its mute and ominous prophecy,
A portent seeming less than threat,
It sank from sight before it set.
A chill no coat, however stout,
Of homespun stuff could quite shut out,   *10*
A hard, dull bitterness of cold,
That checked, mid-vein, the circling race
Of life-blood in the sharpened face,
The coming of the snow-storm told.
The wind blew east; we heard the roar

Of Ocean on his wintry shore,
And felt the strong pulse throbbing there
Beat with low rhythm our inland air.

Meanwhile we did our nightly chores, —
Brought in the wood from out of doors,　　　*20*
Littered the stalls, and from the mows
Raked down the herd's-grass for the cows:
Heard the horse whinnying for his corn;
And, sharply clashing horn on horn,
Impatient down the stanchion rows
The cattle shake their walnut bows;
While, peering from his early perch
Upon the scaffold's pole of birch,
The cock his crested helmet bent
And down his querulous challenge sent.　　*30*

Unwarmed by any sunset light
The gray day darkened into night,
A night made hoary with the swarm,
And whirl-dance of the blinding storm,
As zigzag, wavering to and fro,
Crossed and recrossed the wingëd snow:
And ere the early bedtime came
The white drift piled the window-frame,
And through the glass the clothes-line posts
Looked in like tall and sheeted ghosts.　　*40*

So all night long the storm roared on:
The morning broke without a sun;
In tiny spherule traced with lines
Of Nature's geometric signs,
In starry flake, and pellicle,
All day the hoary meteor fell;
And, when the second morning shone,
We looked upon a world unknown,
On nothing we could call our own.
Around the glistening wonder bent　　　*50*
The blue walls of the firmament,
No cloud above, no earth below, —
A universe of sky and snow!
The old familiar sights of ours

169

Took marvellous shapes; strange domes and
    towers
Rose up where sty or corn-crib stood,
Or garden-wall, or belt of wood;
A smooth white mound the brush-pile showed,
A fenceless drift what once was road;
The bridle-post an old man sat   *60*
With loose-flung coat and high cocked hat;
The well-curb had a Chinese roof;
And even the long sweep, high aloof,
In its slant splendor, seemed to tell
Of Pisa's leaning miracle.

A prompt, decisive man, no breath
Our father wasted: "Boys, a path!"
Well pleased, (for when did farmer boy
Count such a summons less than joy?)
Our buskins on our feet we drew;   *70*
With mittened hands, and caps drawn low,
To guard our necks and ears from snow,
We cut the solid whiteness through.
And, where the drift was deepest, made
A tunnel walled and overlaid
With dazzling crystal: we had read
Of rare Aladdin's wondrous cave,
And to our own his name we gave,
With many a wish the luck were ours
To test his lamp's supernal powers.   *80*
We reached the barn with merry din,
And roused the prisoned brutes within.
The old horse thrust his long head out,
And grave with wonder gazed about;
The cock his lusty greeting said,
And forth his speckled harem led;
The oxen lashed their tails, and hooked,
And mild reproach of hunger looked;
The hornëd patriarch of the sheep,
Like Egypt's Amun roused from sleep,   *90*
Shook his sage head with gesture mute,
And emphasized with stamp of foot.

All day the gusty north-wind bore

The loosening drift its breath before;
Low circling round its southern zone,
The sun through dazzling snow-mist shone.
No church-bell lent its Christian tone
To the savage air, no social smoke
Curled over woods of snow-hung oak.
A solitude made more intense   *100*
By dreary-voicëd elements,
The shrieking of the mindless wind,
The moaning tree-boughs swaying blind,
And on the glass the unmeaning beat
Of ghostly finger-tips of sleet.
Beyond the circle of our hearth
No welcome sound of toil or mirth
Unbound the spell, and testified
Of human life and thought outside.
We minded that the sharpest ear   *110*
The buried brooklet could not hear,
The music of whose liquid lip
Had been to us companionship,
And, in our lonely life, had grown
To have an almost human tone.

As night drew on, and, from the crest
Of wooded knolls that ridged the west,
The sun, a snow-blown traveller, sank
From sight beneath the smothering bank,
We piled, with care, our nightly stack   *120*
Of wood against the chimney-back, —
The oaken log, green, huge, and thick,
And on its top the stout back-stick;
The knotty forestick laid apart,
And filled between with curious art
The ragged brush; then, hovering near,
We watched the first red blaze appear,
Heard the sharp crackle, caught the gleam
On whitewashed wall and sagging beam,
Until the old, rude-furnished room   *130*
Burst, flower-like, into rosy bloom;
While radiant with a mimic flame
Outside the sparkling drift became,
And through the bare-boughed lilac-tree

Our own warm hearth seemed blazing free.
The crane and pendent trammels showed,
The Turks' heads on the andirons glowed;
While childish fancy, prompt to tell
The meaning of the miracle,
Whispered the old rhyme: "*Under the tree,*   *140*
When fire outdoors burns merrily,
There the witches are making tea."

The moon above the eastern wood
Shone at its full; the hill-range stood
Transfigured in the silver flood,
Its blown snows flashing cold and keen,
Dead white, save where some sharp ravine
Took shadow, or the sombre green
Of hemlocks turned to pitchy black
Against the whiteness at their back.   *150*
For such a world and such a night
Most fitting that unwarming light,
Which only seemed where'er it fell
To make the coldness visible.

Shut in from all the world without,
We sat the clean-winged hearth about,
Content to let the north-wind roar
In baffled rage at pane and door,
While the red logs before us beat
The frost-line back with tropic heat;   *160*
And ever, when a louder blast
Shook beam and rafter as it passed,
The merrier up its roaring draught
The great throat of the chimney laughed;
The house-dog on his paws outspread
Laid to the fire his drowsy head,
The cat's dark silhouette on the wall
A couchant tiger's seemed to fall;
And, for the winter fireside meet,
Between the andirons' straddling feet,   *170*
The mug of cider simmered slow,
The apples sputtered in a row,
And, close at hand, the basket stood
With nuts from brown October's wood.

What matter how the night behaved?
What matter how the north-wind raved?
Blow high, blow low, not all its snow
Could quench our hearth-fire's ruddy glow.
O Time and Change! — with hair as gray
As was my sire's that winter day,   *180*
How strange it seems, with so much gone
Of life and love, to still live on!
Ah, brother! only I and thou
Are left of all that circle now, —
The dear home faces whereupon
That fitful firelight paled and shone.
Henceforward, listen as we will,
The voices of that hearth are still;
Look where we may, the wide earth o'er
Those lighted faces smile no more.   *190*
We tread the paths their feet have worn,
    We sit beneath their orchard trees,
    We hear, like them, the hum of bees
And rustle of the bladed corn;
We turn the pages that they read,
    Their written words we linger o'er,
But in the sun they cast no shade,
No voice is heard, no sign is made,
    No step is on the conscious floor!
Yet Love will dream, and Faith will trust,   *200*
(Since He who knows our need is just,)
That somehow, somewhere, meet we must.
Alas for him who never sees
The stars shine through his cypress-trees!
Who, hopeless, lays his dead away,
Nor looks to see the breaking day
Across the mournful marbles play!
Who hath not learned, in hours of faith,
    The truth to flesh and sense unknown,
That Life is ever lord of Death,   *210*
    And Love can never lose its own!

We sped the time with stories old,
Wrought puzzles out, and riddles told,
Or stammered from our school-book lore
"The Chief of Gambia's golden shore."

How often since, when all the land
Was clay in Slavery's shaping hand,
As if a far-blown trumpet stirred
The languorous sin-sick air, I heard:
"Does not the voice of reason cry,   220
    Claim the first right which Nature gave,
From the red scourge of bondage fly,
    Nor deign to live a burdened slave!"
Our father rode again his ride
On Memphremagog's wooded side;
Sat down again to moose and samp
In trapper's hut and Indian camp;
Lived o'er the old idyllic ease
Beneath St. François' hemlock-trees;
Again for him the moonlight shone   230
On Norman cap and bodiced zone;
Again he heard the violin play
Which led the village dance away,
And mingled in its merry whirl
The grandam and the laughing girl.
Or, nearer home, our steps he led
Where Salisbury's level marshes spread
    Mile-wide as flies the laden bee;
Where merry mowers, hale and strong,
Swept, scythe on scythe, their swaths along   240
    The low green prairies of the sea.
We shared the fishing off Boar's Head,
    And round the rocky Isles of Shoals
    The hake-broil on the drift-wood coals;
The chowder on the sand-beach made,
Dipped by the hungry, steaming hot,
With spoons of clam-shells from the pot.
We heard the tales of witchcraft old,
And dream and sign and marvel told
To sleepy listeners as they lay   250
Stretched idly on the salted hay,
Adrift along the winding shores,
When favoring breezes deigned to blow
The square sail of the gundelow
And idle lay the useless oars.

Our mother, while she turned her wheel
Or run the new-knit stocking-heel,
Told how the Indian hordes came down
At midnight on Cocheco town,
And how her own great-uncle bore   *260*
His cruel scalp-mark to fourscore.
Recalling, in her fitting phrase,
    So rich and picturesque and free,
    (The common unrhymed poetry
Of simple life and country ways,)
The story of her early days, —
She made us welcome to her home;
Old hearths grew wide to give us room;
We stole with her a frightened look
At the gray wizard's conjuring-book,   *270*
The fame whereof went far and wide
Through all the simple country side;
We heard the hawks at twilight play,
The boat-horn on Piscataqua,
The loon's weird laughter far away;
We fished her little trout-brook, knew
What flowers in wood and meadow grew,
What sunny hillsides autumn-brown
She climbed to shake the ripe nuts down,
Saw where in sheltered cove and bay   *280*
The ducks' black squadron anchored lay,
And heard the wild geese calling loud
Beneath the gray November cloud.

Then, haply, with a look more grave,
And soberer tone, some tale she gave
From painful Sewell's ancient tome,
Beloved in every Quaker home,
Of faith fire-winged by martyrdom,
Or Chalkley's Journal, old and quaint, —
Gentlest of skippers, rare sea-saint! —   *290*
Who, when the dreary calms prevailed,
And water-butt and bread-cask failed,
And cruel, hungry eyes pursued
His portly presence mad for food,

With dark hints muttered under breath
Of casting lots for life or death,
Offered, if Heaven withheld supplies,
To be himself the sacrifice.
Then, suddenly, as if to save
The good man from his living grave,   *300*
A ripple on the water grew,
A school of porpoise flashed in view.
"Take, eat," he said, "and be content;
These fishes in my stead are sent
By Him who gave the tangled ram
To spare the child of Abraham."

Our uncle, innocent of books,
Was rich in lore of fields and brooks,
The ancient teachers never dumb
Of Nature's unhoused lyceum.   *310*
In moons and tides and weather wise,
He read the clouds as prophecies,
And foul or fair could well divine,
By many an occult hint and sign,
Holding the cunning-warded keys
To all the woodcraft mysteries;
Himself to Nature's heart so near
That all her voices in his ear
Of beast or bird had meanings clear,
Like Apollonius of old,   *320*
Who knew the tales the sparrows told,
Or Hermes who interpreted
What the sage cranes of Nilus said;
Content to live where life began;
A simple, guileless, childlike man,
Strong only on his native grounds,
The little world of sights and sounds
Whose girdle was the parish bounds,
Whereof his fondly partial pride
The common features magnified,   *330*
As Surrey hills to mountains grew
In White of Selborne's loving view,—
He told how teal and loon he shot,
And how the eagle's eggs he got,

The feats on pond and river done,
The prodigies of rod and gun;
Till, warming with the tales he told,
Forgotten was the outside cold,
The bitter wind unheeded blew,
From ripening corn the pigeons flew,   *340*
The partridge drummed i' the wood, the mink
Went fishing down the river-brink.
In fields with bean or clover gay,
The woodchuck, like a hermit gray,
   Peered from the doorway of his cell;
The muskrat plied the mason's trade,
And tier by tier his mud-walls laid;
And from the shagbark overhead
   The grizzled squirrel dropped his shell.

Next, the dear aunt, whose smile of cheer   *350*
And voice in dreams I see and hear, —
The sweetest woman ever Fate
Perverse denied a household mate,
Who, lonely, homeless, not the less
Found peace in love's unselfishness,
And welcome wheresoe'er she went,
A calm and gracious element,
Whose presence seemed the sweet income
And womanly atmosphere of home, —
Called up her girlhood memories,   *360*
The huskings and the apple-bees,
The sleigh-rides and the summer sails,
Weaving through all the poor details
And homespun warp of circumstance
A golden woof-thread of romance.
For well she kept her genial mood
And simple faith of maidenhood;
Before her still a cloud-land lay,
The mirage loomed across her way;
The morning dew, that dries so soon   *370*
With others, glistened at her noon;
Through years of toil and soil and care
From glossy tress to thin gray hair,
All unprofaned she held apart

The virgin fancies of the heart.
Be shame to him of woman born
Who hath for such but thought of scorn.

There, too, our elder sister plied
Her evening task the stand beside;
A full, rich nature, free to trust,   *380*
Truthful and almost sternly just,
Impulsive, earnest, prompt to act,
And make her generous thought a fact,
Keeping with many a light disguise
The secret of self-sacrifice.
O heart sore-tried! thou hast the best
That Heaven itself could give thee, — rest,
Rest from all bitter thoughts and things!
    How many a poor one's blessing went
    With thee beneath the low green tent   *390*
Whose curtain never outward swings!

As one who held herself a part
Of all she saw, and let her heart
    Against the household bosom lean,
Upon the motley-braided mat
Our youngest and our dearest sat,
Lifting her large, sweet, asking eyes,
    Now bathed in the unfading green
And holy peace of Paradise.
Oh, looking from some heavenly hill,   *400*
    Or from the shade of saintly palms,
    Or silver reach of river calms,
Do those large eyes behold me still?
With me one little year ago: —
The chill weight of the winter snow
    For months upon her grave has lain;
And now, when summer south-winds blow
    And brier and harebell bloom again,
I tread the pleasant paths we trod,
I see the violet-sprinkled sod   *410*
Whereon she leaned, too frail and weak
The hillside flowers she loved to seek,
Yet following me where'er I went
With dark eyes full of love's content.

The birds are glad; the brier-rose fills
The air with sweetness; all the hills
Stretch green to June's unclouded sky;
But still I wait with ear and eye
For something gone which should be nigh,
A loss in all familiar things,   *420*
In flower that blooms, and bird that sings.
And yet, dear heart! remembering thee,
   Am I not richer than of old?
Safe in thy immortality,
    What change can reach the wealth I hold?
    What chance can mar the pearl and gold
Thy love hath left in trust with me?
And while in life's late afternoon,
   Where cool and long the shadows grow,
I walk to meet the night that soon   *430*
   Shall shape and shadow overflow,
I cannot feel that thou art far,
Since near at need the angels are;
And when the sunset gates unbar,
   Shall I not see thee waiting stand,
And, white against the evening star,
   The welcome of thy beckoning hand?

Brisk wielder of the birch and rule,
The master of the district school
Held at the fire his favored place,   *440*
Its warm glow lit a laughing face
Fresh-hued and fair, where scarce appeared
The uncertain prophecy of beard.
He teased the mitten-blinded cat,
Played cross-pins on my uncle's hat,
Sang songs, and told us what befalls
In classic Dartmouth's college halls.
Born the wild Northern hills among,
From whence his yeoman father wrung
By patient toil subsistence scant,   *450*
Not competence and yet not want,
He early gained the power to pay
His cheerful, self-reliant way;
Could doff at ease his scholar's gown
To peddle wares from town to town;

Or through the long vacation's reach
In lonely lowland districts teach,
Where all the droll experience found
At stranger hearths in boarding round,
The moonlit skater's keen delight,   *460*
The sleigh-drive through the frosty night,
The rustic party, with its rough
Accompaniment of blind-man's-buff,
And whirling plate, and forfeits paid,
His winter task a pastime made.
Happy the snow-locked homes wherein
He tuned his merry violin,
Or played the athlete in the barn,
Or held the good dame's winding-yarn,
Or mirth-provoking versions told   *470*
Of classic legends rare and old,
Wherein the scenes of Greece and Rome
Had all the commonplace of home,
And little seemed at best the odds
'Twixt Yankee pedlers and old gods;
Where Pindus-born Arachthus took
The guise of any grist-mill brook,
And dread Olympus at his will
Became a huckleberry hill.

A careless boy that night he seemed;   *480*
  But at his desk he had the look
And air of one who wisely schemed,
  And hostage from the future took
  In trainëd thought and lore of book.
Large-brained, clear-eyed, of such as he
Shall Freedom's young apostles be,
Who, following in War's bloody trail,
Shall every lingering wrong assail;
All chains from limb and spirit strike,
Uplift the black and white alike;   *490*
Scatter before their swift advance
The darkness and the ignorance,
The pride, the lust, the squalid sloth,
Which nurtured Treason's monstrous growth,
Made murder pastime, and the hell
Of prison-torture possible;

The cruel lie of caste refute,
Old forms remould, and substitute
For Slavery's lash the freeman's will,
For blind routine, wise-handed skill;   *500*
A school-house plant on every hill,
Stretching in radiate nerve-lines thence
The quick wires of intelligence;
Till North and South together brought
Shall own the same electric thought,
In peace a common flag salute,
And, side by side in labor's free
And unresentful rivalry,
Harvest the fields wherein they fought.

Another guest that winter night   *510*
Flashed back from lustrous eyes the light.
Unmarked by time, and yet not young,
The honeyed music of her tongue
And words of meekness scarcely told
A nature passionate and bold,
Strong, self-concentred, spurning guide,
Its milder features dwarfed beside
Her unbent will's majestic pride.
She sat among us, at the best,
A not unfeared, half-welcome guest,   *520*
Rebuking with her cultured phrase
Our homeliness of words and ways.
A certain pard-like, treacherous grace
    Swayed the lithe limbs and dropped the lash,
    Lent the white teeth their dazzling flash;
    And under low brows, black with night,
    Rayed out at times a dangerous light;
The sharp heat-lightnings of her face
Presaging ill to him whom Fate
Condemned to share her love or hate.   *530*
A woman tropical, intense
In thought and act, in soul and sense,
She blended in a like degree
The vixen and the devotee,
Revealing with each freak or feint
    The temper of Petruchio's Kate,
The raptures of Siena's saint.

181

Her tapering hand and rounded wrist
Had facile power to form a fist;
The warm, dark languish of her eyes   *540*
Was never safe from wrath's surprise.
Brows saintly calm and lips devout
Knew every change of scowl and pout;
And the sweet voice had notes more high
And shrill for social battle-cry.

Since then what old cathedral town
Has missed her pilgrim staff and gown,
What convent-gate has held its lock
Against the challenge of her knock!
Through Smyrna's plague-hushed
     thoroughfares,   *550*
Up sea-set Malta's rocky stairs,
Gray olive slopes of hills that hem
  Thy tombs and shrines, Jerusalem,
Or startling on her desert throne
The crazy Queen of Lebanon
With claims fantastic as her own,
Her tireless feet have held their way;
And still, unrestful, bowed, and gray,
She watches under Eastern skies,
  With hope each day renewed and fresh,   *560*
  The Lord's quick coming in the flesh,
Whereof she dreams and prophesies!

Where'er her troubled path may be,
  The Lord's sweet pity with her go!
The outward wayward life we see,
  The hidden springs we may not know.
Nor is it given us to discern
  What threads the fatal sisters spun,
  Through what ancestral years has run
The sorrow with the woman born,   *570*
What forged her cruel chain of moods,
What set her feet in solitudes,
  And held the love within her mute,
What mingled madness in the blood,
  A life-long discord and annoy,
  Water of tears with oil of joy,

And hid within the folded bud
   Perversities of flower and fruit.
It is not ours to separate
   The tangled skein of will and fate,   580
To show what metes and bounds should stand
Upon the soul's debatable land,
And between choice and Providence
Divide the circle of events;
But He who knows our frame is just,
Merciful and compassionate,
And full of sweet assurances
And hope for all the language is,
That He remembereth we are dust!

At last the great logs, crumbling low,   590
Sent out a dull and duller glow,
The bull's-eye watch that hung in view,
Ticking its weary circuit through,
Pointed with mutely warning sign
Its black hand to the hour of nine.
That sign the pleasant circle broke:
My uncle ceased his pipe to smoke,
Knocked from its bowl the refuse gray,
And laid it tenderly away,
Then roused himself to safely cover   600
The dull red brands with ashes over.
And while, with care, our mother laid
The work aside, her steps she stayed
One moment, seeking to express
Her grateful sense of happiness
For food and shelter, warmth and health,
And love's contentment more than wealth,
With simple wishes (not the weak,
Vain prayers which no fulfilment seek,
But such as warm the generous heart,   610
O'er-prompt to do with Heaven its part)
That none might lack, that bitter night,
For bread and clothing, warmth and light.

Within our beds awhile we heard
The wind that round the gables roared,
With now and then a ruder shock,

Which made our very bedsteads rock.
We heard the loosened clapboards tost,
The board-nails snapping in the frost;
And on us, through the unplastered wall,   *620*
Felt the light sifted snow-flakes fall.
But sleep stole on, as sleep will do
When hearts are light and life is new;
Faint and more faint the murmurs grew,
Till in the summer-land of dreams
They softened to the sound of streams,
Low stir of leaves, and dip of oars,
And lapsing waves on quiet shores.

Next morn we wakened with the shout
Of merry voices high and clear;   *630*
And saw the teamsters drawing near
To break the drifted highways out.
Down the long hillside treading slow
We saw the half-buried oxen go,
Shaking the snow from heads uptost,
Their straining nostrils white with frost.
Before our door the straggling train
Drew up, an added team to gain.
The elders threshed their hands a-cold,
    Passed, with the cider-mug, their jokes *640*
    From lip to lip; the younger folks
Down the loose snow-banks, wrestling, rolled,
Then toiled again the cavalcade
    O'er windy hill, through clogged ravine,
    And woodland paths that wound between
Low drooping pine-boughs winter-weighed.
From every barn a team afoot,
At every house a new recruit,
Where, drawn by Nature's subtlest law
Haply the watchful young men saw   *650*
Sweet doorway pictures of the curls
And curious eyes of merry girls,
Lifting their hands in mock defence
Against the snow-ball's compliments,
And reading in each missive tost
The charm with Eden never lost.

We heard once more the sleigh-bells' sound;
    And, following where the teamsters led,
The wise old Doctor went his round,
Just pausing at our door to say,   *660*
In the brief autocratic way
Of one who, prompt at Duty's call,
Was free to urge her claim on all,
    That some poor neighbor sick abed
At night our mother's aid would need.
For, one in generous thought and deed,
    What mattered in the sufferer's sight
    The Quaker matron's inward light,
The Doctor's mail of Calvin's creed?
All hearts confess the saints elect   *670*
    Who, twain in faith, in love agree,
And melt not in an acid sect
    The Christian pearl of charity!

So days went on: a week had passed
Since the great world was heard from last.
The Almanac we studied o'er,
Read and reread our little store,
Of books and pamphlets, scarce a score;
One harmless novel, mostly hid
From younger eyes, a book forbid,   *680*
And poetry, (or good or bad,
A single book was all we had,)
Where Ellwood's meek, drab-skirted Muse,
    A stranger to the heathen Nine,
    Sang, with a somewhat nasal whine,
The wars of David and the Jews.
At last the floundering carrier bore
The village paper to our door.
Lo! broadening outward as we read,
To warmer zones the horizon spread;   *690*
In panoramic length unrolled
We saw the marvels that it told.
Before us passed the painted Creeks,
    And daft McGregor on his raids
    In Costa Rica's everglades.
And up Taygetos winding slow

185

Rode Ypsilanti's Mainote Greeks,
A Turk's head at each saddle-bow!
Welcome to us its week-old news,
Its corner for the rustic Muse,   *700*
    Its monthly gauge of snow and rain,
Its record, mingling in a breath
The wedding bell and dirge of death;
Jest, anecdote, and love-lorn tale,
The latest culprit sent to jail;
Its hue and cry of stolen and lost,
Its vendue sales and goods at cost,
    And traffic calling loud for gain.
We felt the stir of hall and street,
The pulse of life that round us beat;   *710*
The chill embargo of the snow
Was melted in the genial glow;
Wide swung again our ice-locked door,
And all the world was ours once more!

Clasp, Angel of the backward look
    And folded wings of ashen gray
    And voice of echoes far away,
The brazen covers of thy book;
The weird palimpsest old and vast,
Wherein thou hid'st the spectral past;   *720*
Where, closely mingling, pale and glow
The characters of joy and woe;
The monographs of outlived years,
Or smile-illumed or dim with tears,
    Green hills of life that slope to death,
And haunts of home, whose vistaed trees
Shade off to mournful cypresses
    With the white amaranths underneath.
Even while I look, I can but heed
    The restless sands' incessant fall,   *730*
Importunate hours that hours succeed,
Each clamorous with its own sharp need,
    And duty keeping pace with all.
Shut down and clasp the heavy lids;
I hear again the voice that bids
The dreamer leave his dream midway
For larger hopes and graver fears:

Life greatens in these later years,
The century's aloe flowers to-day!

Yet, haply, in some lull of life,   *740*
Some Truce of God which breaks its strife,
The worldling's eyes shall gather dew,
    Dreaming in throngful city ways
Of winter joys his boyhood knew;
And dear and early friends — the few
Who yet remain — shall pause to view
    These Flemish pictures of old days;
Sit with me by the homestead hearth,
And stretch the hands of memory forth
    To warm them at the wood-fire's blaze!   *750*
And thanks untraced to lips unknown
Shall greet me like the odors blown
From unseen meadows newly mown,
Or lilies floating in some pond,
Wood-fringed, the wayside gaze beyond;
The traveller owns the grateful sense
Of sweetness near, he knows not whence,
And, pausing, takes with forehead bare
The benediction of the air.

1866.

Abraham Davenport

The famous Dark Day of New England, May 19, 1780, was a physical puzzle for many years to our ancestors, but its occurrence brought something more than philosophical speculation into the minds of those who passed through it. The incident of Colonel Abraham Davenport's sturdy protest is a matter of history.

In the old days (a custom laid aside
With breeches and cocked hats) the people sent
Their wisest men to make the public laws.
And so, from a brown homestead, where the Sound
Drinks the small tribute of the Mianas,
Waved over by the woods of Rippowams,
And hallowed by pure lives and tranquil deaths,
Stamford sent up to the councils of the State
Wisdom and grace in Abraham Davenport.

'T was on a May-day of the far old year
Seventeen hundred eighty, that there fell
Over the bloom and sweet life of the Spring,
Over the fresh earth and the heaven of noon,
A horror of great darkness, like the night
In day of which the Norland sagas tell, —
The Twilight of the Gods. The low-hung sky
Was black with ominous clouds, save where its rim
Was fringed with a dull glow, like that which climbs
The crater's sides from the red hell below.
Birds ceased to sing, and all the barn-yard fowls
Roosted; the cattle at the pasture bars
Lowed, and looked homeward; bats on leathern
    wings
Flitted abroad; the sounds of labor died;
Men prayed, and women wept; all ears grew sharp
To hear the doom-blast of the trumpet shatter

The black sky, that the dreadful face of Christ
Might look from the rent clouds, not as he looked
A loving guest at Bethany, but stern
As Justice and inexorable Law.

Meanwhile in the old State House, dim as ghosts,
Sat the lawgivers of Connecticut,
Trembling beneath their legislative robes.
"It is the Lord's Great Day! Let us adjourn,"
Some said; and then, as if with one accord,
All eyes were turned to Abraham Davenport.
He rose, slow cleaving with his steady voice
The intolerable hush. "This well may be
The Day of Judgment which the world awaits;
But be it so or not, I only know
My present duty, and my Lord's command
To occupy till He come. So at the post
Where He hath set me in His providence,
I choose, for one, to meet Him face to face,
No faithless servant frightened from my task,
But ready when the Lord of the harvest calls;
And therefore, with all reverence, I would say,
Let God do His work, we will see to ours.
Bring in the candles." And they brought them in.

Then by the flaring lights the Speaker read,
Albeit with husky voice and shaking hands,
An act to amend an act to regulate
The shad and alewive fisheries. Wherepon
Wisely and well spake Abraham Davenport,
Straight to the question, with no figures of speech
Save the ten Arab signs, yet not without
The shrewd dry humor natural to the man:
His awe-struck colleagues listening all the while,
Between the pauses of his argument,
To hear the thunder of the wrath of God
Break from the hollow trumpet of the cloud.

And there he stands in memory to this day,
Erect, self-poised, a rugged face, half seen
Against the background of unnatural dark,
A witness to the ages as they pass,
That simple duty hath no place for fear.

1866.

The Hive at Gettysburg

In the old Hebrew myth the lion's frame,
   So terrible alive,
Bleached by the desert's sun and wind, became
   The wandering wild bees' hive;
And he who, lone and naked-handed, tore
   Those jaws of death apart,
In after time drew forth their honeyed store
   To strengthen his strong heart.

Dead seemed the legend: but it only slept
   To wake beneath our sky;
Just on the spot whence ravening Treason crept
   Back to its lair to die,
Bleeding and torn from Freedom's mountain
     bounds,
   A stained and shattered drum
Is now the hive where, on their flowery rounds,
   The wild bees go and come.

Unchallenged by a ghostly sentinel,
   They wander wide and far,
Along green hillsides, sown with shot and shell,
   Through vales once choked with war.
The low reveille of their battle-drum
   Disturbs no morning prayer;
With deeper peace in summer noons their hum
   Fills all the drowsy air.

And Samson's riddle is our own to-day,
   Of sweetness from the strong,
Of union, peace, and freedom plucked away
   From the rent jaws of wrong.
From Treason's death we draw a purer life,
   As, from the beast he slew,
A sweetness sweeter for his bitter strife
   The old-time athlete drew!

1868.

191

Prelude from
Among the Hills

This poem, when originally published, was dedicated to Annie Fields, wife of the distinguished publisher, James T. Fields, of Boston, in grateful acknowledgment of the strength and inspiration I have found in her friendship and sympathy.

The poem in its first form was entitled *The Wife: an Idyl of Bear-camp Water*, and appeared in *The Atlantic Monthly* for January, 1868. When I published the volume *Among the Hills*, in December of the same year, I expanded the Prelude and filled out also the outlines of the story.

Along the roadside, like the flowers of gold
That tawny Incas for their gardens wrought,
Heavy with sunshine droops the golden-rod,
And the red pennons of the cardinal-flowers
Hang motionless upon their upright staves.
The sky is hot and hazy, and the wind,
Wing-weary with its long flight from the south,
Unfelt; yet, closely scanned, yon maple leaf
With faintest motion, as one stirs in dreams,
Confesses it. The locust by the wall
Stabs the noon-silence with his sharp alarm.
A single hay-cart down the dusty road
Creaks slowly, with its driver fast asleep
On the load's top. Against the neighboring hill,
Huddled along the stone wall's shady side,
The sheep show white, as if a snowdrift still
Defied the dog-star. Through the open door
A drowsy smell of flowers — gray heliotrope,
And white sweet clover, and shy mignonette —
Comes faintly in, and silent chorus lends
To the pervading symphony of peace.

No time is this for hands long over-worn
To task their strength: and (unto Him be praise

Who giveth quietness!) the stress and strain
Of years that did the work of centuries
Have ceased, and we can draw our breath once
       more
Freely and full. So, as yon harvesters
Make glad their nooning underneath the elms
With tale and riddle and old snatch of song,
I lay aside grave themes, and idly turn
The leaves of memory's sketch-book, dreaming
       o'er
Old summer pictures of the quiet hills,
And human life, as quiet, at their feet.

And yet not idly all. A farmer's son,
Proud of field-lore and harvest craft, and feeling
All their fine possibilities, how rich
And restful even poverty and toil
Become when beauty, harmony, and love
Sit at their humble hearth as angels sat
At evening in the patriarch's tent, when man
Makes labor noble, and his farmer's frock
The symbol of a Christian chivalry
Tender and just and generous to her
Who clothes with grace all duty; still, I know
Too well the picture has another side, —
How wearily the grind of toil goes on
Where love is wanting, how the eye and ear
And heart are starved amidst the plenitude
Of nature, and how hard and colorless
Is life without an atmosphere. I look
Across the lapse of half a century,
And call to mind old homesteads, where no flower
Told that the spring had come, but evil weeds,
Nightshade and rough-leaved burdock in the place
Of the sweet doorway greeting of the rose
And honeysuckle, where the house walls seemed
Blistering in sun, without a tree or vine
To cast the tremulous shadow of its leaves
Across the curtainless windows, from whose
       panes
Fluttered the signal rags of shiftlessness.
Within, the cluttered kitchen-floor, unwashed

(Broom-clean I think they called it); the best
    room
Stifling with cellar damp, shut from the air
In hot midsummer, bookless, pictureless
Save the inevitable sampler hung
Over the fireplace, or a mourning piece,
A green-haired woman, peony-cheeked, beneath
Impossible willows; the wide-throated hearth
Bristling with faded pine-boughs half concealing
The piled-up rubbish at the chimney's back;
And, in sad keeping with all things about them,
Shrill, querulous women, sour and sullen men,
Untidy, loveless, old before their time,
With scarce a human interest save their own
Monotonous round of small economies,
Or the poor scandal of the neighborhood;
Blind to the beauty everywhere revealed,
Treading the May-flowers with regardless feet;
For them the song-sparrow and the bobolink
Sang not, nor winds made music in the leaves;
For them in vain October's holocaust
Burned, gold and crimson, over all the hills,
The sacramental mystery of the woods.
Church-goers, fearful of the unseen Powers,
But grumbling over pulpit-tax and pew-rent,
Saving, as shrewd economists, their souls
And winter pork with the least possible outlay
Of salt and sanctity; in daily life
Showing as little actual comprehension
Of Christian charity and love and duty,
As if the Sermon on the Mount had been
Outdated like a last year's almanac:
Rich in broad woodlands and in half-tilled fields,
And yet so pinched and bare and comfortless,
The veriest straggler limping on his rounds,
The sun and air his sole inheritance,
Laughed at a poverty that paid its taxes,
And hugged his rags in self-complacency!

Not such should be the homesteads of a land
Where whoso wisely wills and acts may dwell
As king and lawgiver, in broad-acred state,

With beauty, art, taste, culture, books, to make
His hour of leisure richer than a life
Of fourscore to the barons of old time,
Our yeoman should be equal to his home
Set in the fair, green valleys, purple walled,
A man to match his mountains, not to creep
Dwarfed and abased below them. I would fain
In this light way (of which I needs must own
With the knife-grinder of whom Canning sings,
"Story, God bless you! I have none to tell you!")
Invite the eye to see and heart to feel
The beauty and the joy within their reach, —
Home, and home loves, and the beatitudes
Of nature free to all. Haply in years
That wait to take the places of our own,
Heard where some breezy balcony looks down
On happy homes, or where the lake in the moon
Sleeps dreaming of the mountains, fair as Ruth,
In the old Hebrew pastoral, at the feet
Of Boaz, even this simple lay of mine
May seem the burden of a prophecy,
Finding its late fulfilment in a change
Slow as the oak's growth, lifting manhood up
Through broader culture, finer manners, love,
And reverence, to the level of the hills.

1869.

In School-Days

Still sits the school-house by the road,
　A ragged beggar sleeping;
And it still the sumachs grow,
　And blackberry-vines are creeping.

Within, the master's desk is seen,
　Deep scarred by raps official;
The warping floor, the battered seats,
　The jack-knife's carved initial;

The charcoal frescos on its wall;
　Its door's worn sill, betraying
The feet that, creeping slow to school,
　Went storming out to playing!

Long years ago a winter sun
　Shown over it at setting;
Lit up its western window-panes,
　And low eaves' icy fretting.

It touched the tangled golden curls,
　And brown eyes full of grieving,
Of one who still her steps delayed
　When all the school were leaving.

For near her stood the little boy
　Her childish favor singled:
His cap pulled low upon a face
　Where pride and shame were mingled.

Pushing with restless feet the snow
　To right and left, he lingered: —
As restlessly her tiny hands
　The blue-checked apron fingered.

He saw her lift her eyes; he felt
   The soft hand's light caressing,
And heard the tremble of her voice,
   As if a fault confessing.

"I'm sorry that I spelt the word:
   I hate to go above you,
Because," — the brown eyes lower fell, —
   "Because you see, I love you!"

Still memory to a gray-haired man
   That sweet child-face is showing.
Dear girl! the grasses on her grave
   Have forty years been growing!

He lives to learn, in life's hard school,
   How few who pass above him
Lament their triumph and his loss,
   Like her, — because they love him.

1870.

The Pressed Gentian

The time of gifts has come again,
And, on my northern window-pane,
Outlined against the day's brief light,
A Christmas token hangs in sight.
The wayside travellers, as they pass,
Mark the gray disk of clouded glass;
And the dull blankness seems, perchance,
Folly to their wise ignorance.

They cannot from their outlook see
The perfect grace it hath for me;
For there the flower, whose fringes through
The frosty breath of autumn blew,
Turns from without its face of bloom
To the warm tropic of my room,
As fair as when beside its brook
The hue of bending skies it took.

So from the trodden ways of earth,
Seem some sweet souls who veil their worth,
And offer to the careless glance
The clouding gray of circumstance.
They blossom best where hearth-fires burn,
To loving eyes alone they turn
The flowers of inward grace, that hide
Their beauty from the world outside.

But deeper meanings come to me,
My half-immortal flower, from thee!
Man judges from a partial view,
None ever yet his brother knew;
The Eternal Eye that sees the whole
May better read the darkened soul,
And find, to outward sense denied,
The flower upon its inmost side!

1872.

Conductor Bradley

A railway conductor who lost his life in an accident on a Connecticut railway, May 9, 1873.

Conductor Bradley, (always may his name
Be said with reverence!) as the swift doom came,
Smitten to death, a crushed and mangled frame,

Sank, with the brake he grasped just where
    he stood
To do the utmost that a brave man could,
And die, if needful, as a true man should.

Men stooped above him; women dropped their
    tears
On that poor wreck beyond all hopes or fears,
Lost in the strength and glory of his years.

What heard they? Lo! the ghastly lips of pain,
Dead to all thought save duty's, moved again:
"Put out the signals for the other train!"

No nobler utterance since the world began
From lips of saint or martyr ever ran,
Electric, through the sympathies of man.

Ah me! how poor and noteless seem to this
The sick-bed dramas of self-consciousness,
Our sensual fears of pain and hopes of bliss!

Oh, grand, supreme endeavor! Not in vain
That last brave act of failing tongue and brain!
Freighted with life the downward rushing train,

Following the wrecked one, as wave follows wave,
Obeyed the warning which the dead lips gave.
Others he saved, himself he could not save.

Nay, the lost life *was* saved. He is not dead
Who in his record still the earth shall tread
With God's clear aureole shining round his head.

We bow as in the dust, with all our pride
Of virtue dwarfed the noble deed beside.
God give us grace to live as Bradley died!

1873.

At Last

When on my day of life the night is falling,
   And, in the winds from unsunned spaces blown,
I hear far voices out of darkness calling
   My feet to paths unknown,

Thou who hast made my home of life so pleasant,
   Leave not its tenant when its walls decay;
O Love Divine, O Helper ever present,
   Be Thou my strength and stay!

Be near me when all else is from me drifting:
   Earth, sky, home's pictures, days of shade and
      shine,
And kindly faces to my own uplifting
   The love which answers mine.

I have but Thee, my Father! let Thy spirit
   Be with me then to comfort and uphold;
No gate of pearl, no branch of palm I merit,
   Nor street of shining gold.

Suffice it if — my good and ill unreckoned,
   And both forgiven through Thy abounding
      grace —
I find myself by hands familiar beckoned
   Unto my fitting place.

Some humble door among Thy many mansions,
   Some sheltering shade where sin and striving
      cease,
And flows forever through heaven's green expan-
      sions
   The river of Thy peace.

There, from the music round about me stealing,
   I fain would learn the new and holy song,
And find at last, beneath Thy trees of healing,
   The life for which I long.

1882.

Abram Morrison

'Midst the men and things which will
Haunt an old man's memory still,
Drollest, quaintest of them all,
With a boy's laugh I recall
  Good old Abram Morrison.

When the Grist and Rolling Mill
Ground and rumbled by Po Hill,
And the old red school-house stood
Midway in the Powow's flood,
  Here dwelt Abram Morrison.

From the Beach to far beyond
Bear-Hill, Lion's Mouth and Pond,
Marvellous to our tough old stock,
Chips o' the Anglo-Saxon block,
  Seemed the Celtic Morrison.

Mudknock, Balmawhistle, all
Only knew the Yankee drawl,
Never brogue was heard till when,
Foremost of his countrymen,
  Hither came Friend Morrison;

Yankee born, of alien blood,
Kin of his had well withstood
Pope and King with pike and ball
Under Derry's leaguered wall,
  As became the Morrisons.

Wandering down from Nutfield woods
With his household and his goods,
Never was it clearly told
How within our quiet fold
  Came to be a Morrison.

Once a soldier, blame him not
That the Quaker he forgot,
When, to think of battles won,
And the red-coats on the run,
        Laughed aloud Friend Morrison.

From gray Lewis over sea
Bore his sires their family tree,
On the rugged boughs of it
Grafting Irish mirth and wit,
        And the brogue of Morrison.

Half a genius, quick to plan,
Blundering like an Irishman,
But with canny shrewdness lent
By his far-off Scotch descent,
        Such was Abram Morrison.

Back and forth to daily meals,
Rode his cherished pig on wheels,
And to all who came to see:
"Aisier for the pig an' me,
        Sure it is," said Morrison.

Simple-hearted, boy o'er-grown,
With a humor quite his own,
Of our sober-stepping ways,
Speech and look and cautious phrase,
        Slow to learn was Morrison.

Much we loved his stories told
Of a country strange and old,
Where the fairies danced till dawn,
And the goblin Leprecaun
        Looked, we thought, like Morrison.

Or wild tales of feud and fight,
Witch and troll and second sight
Whispered still where Stornoway
Looks across its stormy bay,
        Once the home of Morrisons.

First was he to sing the praise
Of the Powow's winding ways;
And our straggling village took
City grandeur to the look
        Of its poet Morrison.

All his words have perished. Shame
On the saddle-bags of Fame,
That they bring not to our time
One poor couplet of the rhyme
        Made by Abram Morrison!

When, on calm and fair First Days,
Rattled down our one-horse chaise,
Through the blossomed apple-boughs
To the old, brown meeting-house,
        There was Abram Morrison.

Underneath his hat's broad brim
Peered the queer old face of him;
And with Irish jauntiness
Swung the coat-tails of the dress
        Worn by Abram Morrison.

Still, in memory, on his feet,
Leaning o'er the elders' seat,
Mingling with a solemn drone,
Celtic accents all his own,
        Rises Abram Morrison.

"Don't," he's pleading, "don't ye go,
Dear young friends, to sight and show,
Don't run after elephants,
Learned pigs and presidents
        And the likes!" said Morrison.

On his well-worn theme intent,
Simple, child-like, innocent,
Heaven forgive the half-checked smile
Of our careless boyhood, while
        Listening to Friend Morrison!

We have learned in later days
Truth may speak in simplest phrase;
That the man is not the less
For quaint ways and home-spun dress,
      Thanks to Abram Morrison!

Not to pander nor to please
Come the needed homilies,
With no lofty argument
Is the fitting message sent,
      Through such lips as Morrison's.

Dead and gone! But while its track
Powow keeps to Merrimac,
While Po Hill is still on guard,
Looking land and ocean ward,
      They shall tell of Morrison!

After half a century's lapse,
We are wiser now, perhaps,
But we miss our streets amid
Something which the past has hid,
      Lost with Abram Morrison.

Gone forever with the queer
Characters of that old year!
Now the many are as one;
Broken is the mould that run
      Men like Abram Morrison.

1884.

On the Big Horn

In the disastrous battle on the Big Horn River, in which General Custer and his entire force were slain, the chief Rain-in-the-Face was one of the fiercest leaders of the Indians. In Longfellow's poem on the massacre, these lines will be remembered: —

> "Revenge!" cried Rain-in-the-Face,
> "Revenge upon all the race
>   Of the White Chief with yellow hair!"
> And the mountains dark and high
> From their crags reëchoed the cry
>   Of his anger and despair.

He is now a man of peace; and the agent at Standing Rock, Dakota, writes, September 28, 1886: "Rain-in-the-Face is very anxious to go to Hampton. I fear he is too old, but he desires very much to go." *The Southern Workman*, the organ of General Armstrong's Industrial School at Hampton, Va., says in a late number: —

"Rain-in-the-Face has applied before to come to Hampton, but his age would exclude him from the school as an ordinary student. He has shown himself very much in earnest about it, and is anxious, all say, to learn the better ways of life. It is as unusual as it is striking to see a man of his age, and one who has had such an experience, willing to give up the old way, and put himself in the position of a boy and a student."

> The years are but half a score,
> And the war-whoop sounds no more
>   With the blast of bugles, where
> Straight into a slaughter pen,
> With his doomed three hundred men,
>   Rode the chief with the yellow hair.
>
> O Hampton, down by the sea!
> What voice is beseeching thee
>   For the scholar's lowliest place?
> Can this be the voice of him
> Who fought on the Big Horn's rim?
>   Can this be Rain-in-the-Face?

His war-paint is washed away,
His hands have forgotten to slay;
 He seeks for himself and his race
The arts of peace and the lore
That give to the skilled hand more
 Than the spoils of war and chase.

O chief of the Christ-like school!
Can the zeal of thy heart grow cool
 When the victor scarred with fight
Like a child for thy guidance craves,
And the faces of hunters and braves
 Are turning to thee for light?

The hatchet lies overgrown
With grass by the Yellowstone,
 Wind River and Paw of Bear;
And, in sign that foes are friends,
Each lodge like a peace-pipe sends
 Its smoke in the quiet air.

The hands that have done the wrong
To right the wronged are strong,
 And the voice of a nation saith:
"Enough of the war of swords,
 Enough of the lying words
 And shame of a broken faith!"

The hills that have watched afar
The valleys ablaze with war
 Shall look on the tasselled corn;
And the dust of the grinded grain,
Instead of the blood of the slain,
 Shall sprinkle thy banks, Big Horn!

The Ute and the wandering Crow
Shall know as the white men know,
 And fare as the white men fare;
The pale and the red shall be brothers,

One's rights shall be as another's,
  Home, School, and House of Prayer!

O mountains that climb to snow,
O river winding below,
  Through meadows by war once trod,
O wild, waste lands that await
The harvest exceeding great,
  Break forth into praise of God!

1887.